Incredibly Easy

Gifts from the Kitchen

Publications International, Ltd.

Favorite Brand Name Recipes at www.fbnr.com

Pictured on the front cover: Apple Cinnamon Chunkies *(page 45)*.

Pictured on the back cover: Fruit Crumble *(page 136)*.

ISBN-13: 978-1-4127-2551-4
ISBN-10: 1-4127-2551-8

Library of Congress Control Number: 2007921111

Manufactured in China.

8 7 6 5 4 3 2 1

Microwave Cooking: Microwave ovens vary in wattage. Use the cooking times as guidelines and check for doneness before adding more time.

Preparation/Cooking Times: Preparation times are based on the approximate amount of time required to assemble the recipe before cooking, baking, chilling or serving. These times include preparation steps such as measuring, chopping and mixing. The fact that some preparations and cooking can be done simultaneously is taken into account. Preparation of optional ingredients and serving suggestions is not included.

Contents

Caramel-Nut Sticky Biscuits
(p. 12)

Lots o' Chocolate Bread
(p. 28)

Irish Soda Bread Rounds
(p. 24)

Blueberry White Chip
Muffins (p. 20)

Breads & Muffins

Quick Pumpkin Bread

1 cup packed light brown sugar
⅓ cup cold butter, cut into 5 pieces
2 eggs
1 cup solid-pack pumpkin
1½ cups all-purpose flour
½ cup whole wheat flour
1½ teaspoons pumpkin pie spice*
1 teaspoon baking soda
¾ teaspoon salt
½ teaspoon baking powder
¼ teaspoon ground cardamom (optional)
½ cup dark raisins or chopped pitted dates
½ cup chopped pecans or walnuts

*A mixture of ¾ teaspoon ground cinnamon, ⅜ teaspoon ground ginger and scant ¼ teaspoon each ground allspice and ground nutmeg can be substituted for 1½ teaspoons pumpkin pie spice.

1. Preheat oven to 350°F. Grease 9×5-inch loaf pan or 3 mini 5×3-inch loaf pans. Fit food processor with steel blade.

2. Measure sugar and butter into work bowl. Process until smooth, about 10 seconds.

3. Turn on processor and add eggs one at a time through feed tube. Add pumpkin, flours, pie spice, baking soda, salt, baking powder and cardamom, if desired. Process just until flour is moistened, about 5 seconds. Do not overprocess. Batter should be lumpy.

4. Sprinkle raisins and nuts over batter. Process using on/off pulsing action 2 or 3 times or just until raisins and nuts are mixed into batter.

5. Turn batter into prepared pan. Bake until toothpick inserted into center comes out clean, about 1 hour for large loaf or 30 to 35 minutes for small loaves. Cool bread in pan 15 minutes. Remove from pan; cool on wire rack.

Makes 1 large or 3 small loaves

Note: Whole wheat flour can be omitted, if desired, and a total of 2 cups all-purpose flour used instead.

Toffee Crunch Muffins

1½ cups all-purpose flour
⅓ cup packed brown sugar
2 teaspoons baking powder
½ teaspoon baking soda
½ teaspoon salt
½ cup milk
½ cup sour cream
1 egg, beaten
3 tablespoons butter, melted
1 teaspoon vanilla
3 bars (1.4 ounces each) chocolate-covered toffee,
    chopped, divided

1. Preheat oven to 400°F. Grease 36 mini (1¾-inch) muffin cups or line with paper baking cups.

2. Combine flour, sugar, baking powder, baking soda and salt in large bowl. Combine milk, sour cream, egg, butter and vanilla in small bowl until well blended. Stir into flour mixture just until moistened. Fold in two thirds of toffee. Spoon batter into prepared muffin cups, filling almost full. Sprinkle evenly with remaining toffee.

3. Bake 16 to 18 minutes or until toothpick inserted into centers comes out clean. Remove from pans; cool on wire racks 10 minutes. Serve warm or cool completely.   *Makes 36 mini muffins*

Variation: For regular-size muffins, spoon batter into 10 standard (2½-inch) greased or paper-lined muffin cups. Bake at 350°F about 20 minutes or until toothpick inserted into centers comes out clean. Makes 10 muffins.

Cinnamon Honey Buns

¼ cup butter or margarine, softened and divided
½ cup honey, divided
¼ cup chopped toasted nuts
2 teaspoons ground cinnamon
1 loaf (1 pound) frozen bread dough, thawed
⅔ cup raisins

Grease 12 muffin cups with 1 tablespoon butter. To prepare honey-nut topping, mix together 1 tablespoon butter, ¼ cup honey and chopped nuts. Place 1 teaspoon topping in each muffin cup. To prepare filling, mix together remaining 2 tablespoons butter, remaining ¼ cup honey and cinnamon. Roll out bread dough on floured surface to 18×8-inch rectangle. Spread filling evenly over dough. Sprinkle with raisins. Starting with long side, roll dough into log. Cut log into 12 (1½-inch) slices. Place 1 slice, cut side up, into each prepared muffin cup. Set muffin pan in warm place; let dough rise 30 minutes. Place muffin pan on foil-lined baking sheet. Bake at 375°F 20 minutes or until buns are golden brown. Cool in pan 5 minutes. Invert muffin pan to remove buns.

Makes 12 buns

Favorite recipe from **National Honey Board**

Cranberry-Cheese Batter Bread

1¼ cups milk
3 cups all-purpose flour
½ cup sugar
1 package (¼ ounce) active dry yeast
1 teaspoon salt
½ cup (1 stick) butter, chilled
½ cup (4 ounces) cream cheese, chilled
1 cup (3 ounces) dried cranberries

1. Grease 8-inch square baking pan; set aside. Heat milk in small saucepan over low heat until temperature reaches 120° to 130°F.

2. Combine flour, sugar, yeast and salt in large bowl. Cut butter and cream cheese into 1-inch chunks; add to flour mixture. Cut in butter and cream cheese with pastry blender until mixture resembles coarse crumbs. Add cranberries; toss. Add warm milk; beat 1 minute or until dough looks stringy. Transfer batter to prepared pan. Cover with towel; let rise in warm place about 1 hour.

3. Preheat oven to 375°F. Bake 35 minutes or until golden brown.

Makes 1 loaf

Caramel-Nut Sticky Biscuits

Topping

    ⅔ **cup firmly packed brown sugar**
    ¼ **cup light corn syrup**
    ¼ **cup (½ stick) margarine, melted**
    ½ **teaspoon ground cinnamon**
    1 **cup pecan halves**

Biscuits

    2 **cups all-purpose flour**
    1 **cup QUAKER® Oats (quick or old fashioned, uncooked)**
    ¼ **cup granulated sugar**
    1 **tablespoon baking powder**
    ¾ **teaspoon baking soda**
    ½ **teaspoon salt (optional)**
    ½ **teaspoon ground cinnamon**
    ⅓ **cup (5⅓ tablespoons) margarine**
    1 **cup buttermilk***

*Sour milk can be substituted for buttermilk. For 1 cup sour milk, combine 1 tablespoon vinegar or lemon juice and enough milk to make 1 cup; let stand 5 minutes.

Heat oven to 425°F. For topping, combine first four ingredients; mix well. Spread onto bottom of 9-inch square baking pan. Sprinkle with pecans; set aside.

For biscuits, combine dry ingredients; mix well. Cut in margarine with pastry blender or two knives until crumbly. Stir in buttermilk, mixing just until moistened. Knead gently on lightly floured surface 5 to 7 times; pat into 8-inch square. Cut with knife into sixteen 2-inch square biscuits; place over topping in pan. Bake 25 to 28 minutes or until golden brown. Let stand 3 minutes; invert onto large platter. Serve warm.

Makes 16 servings

Orange Fruit Bread

2 cups all-purpose flour
¼ cup sugar
1½ teaspoons baking powder
½ teaspoon baking soda
½ teaspoon salt
¼ cup Dried Plum Purée (recipe follows) or prepared dried plum butter
¾ cup orange juice
½ cup orange marmalade
Grated peel of 1 orange
1 package (6 ounces) mixed dried fruit bits
¼ cup chopped toasted pecans

Preheat oven to 350°F. Coat 8½×4½×2¾-inch loaf pan with vegetable cooking spray. In mixer bowl, combine flour, sugar, baking powder, baking soda and salt. Add Dried Plum Purée; beat at low speed until blended. Add juice, marmalade and orange peel. Beat at low speed just until blended. Stir in fruit bits and pecans. Spoon batter into prepared pan. Bake in center of oven about 1 hour or until pick inserted into center comes out clean. Cool in pan 5 minutes; remove from pan to wire rack. Cool completely. For best flavor, wrap securely and store overnight before slicing. Serve with orange marmalade, if desired.

Makes 1 loaf (12 slices)

Dried Plum Purée: Combine 1⅓ cups (8 ounces) pitted dried plums and 6 tablespoons hot water in container of food processor or blender. Pulse on and off until dried plums are finely chopped and smooth. Store leftovers in a covered container in the refrigerator for up to two months. Makes 1 cup.

Favorite recipe from **California Dried Plum Board**

White Chocolate Chunk Muffins

2½ cups all-purpose flour
1 cup packed light brown sugar
⅓ cup unsweetened cocoa powder
2 teaspoons baking soda
½ teaspoon salt
1⅓ cups buttermilk
¼ cup (½ stick) plus 2 tablespoons butter, melted
2 eggs, beaten
1½ teaspoons vanilla
1½ cups chopped white chocolate

1. Preheat oven to 400°F. Grease 12 jumbo (3½-inch) muffin cups.

2. Combine flour, sugar, cocoa, baking soda and salt in large bowl. Combine buttermilk, butter, eggs and vanilla in small bowl until blended. Stir into flour mixture just until moistened. Fold in white chocolate. Spoon into prepared muffin cups, filling each halfway full.

3. Bake 25 to 30 minutes or until toothpick inserted into centers comes out clean. Cool in pan on wire rack 5 minutes. Remove from pan. Cool on wire rack 10 minutes. Serve warm or cool completely.

Makes 12 large muffins

Creamy Cinnamon Rolls

Prep Time: 20 minutes • **Chill Time:** Overnight
Bake Time: 30 to 35 minutes • **Cool Time:** 5 minutes

2 (1-pound) loaves frozen bread dough, thawed
⅔ cup (half of 14-ounce can*) EAGLE BRAND® Sweetened
    Condensed Milk (NOT evaporated milk), divided
1 cup chopped pecans
2 teaspoons ground cinnamon
1 cup confectioners' sugar
½ teaspoon vanilla extract
    Additional chopped pecans (optional)

Use remaining EAGLE BRAND® as a dip for fruit. Pour into storage container and store tightly covered in refrigerator for up to 1 week.

1. On lightly floured surface, roll each bread dough loaf into 12×9-inch rectangle. Spread ⅓ cup EAGLE BRAND® over dough rectangles. Sprinkle rectangles with 1 cup pecans and cinnamon. Roll up jelly-roll-style starting from short side. Cut each log into 6 slices.

2. Generously grease 13×9-inch baking pan. Place rolls, cut sides down, in pan. Cover loosely with greased wax paper and then with plastic wrap. Chill overnight. Cover and chill remaining EAGLE BRAND®.

3. To bake, let pan of rolls stand at room temperature 30 minutes. Preheat oven to 350°F. Bake 30 to 35 minutes or until golden brown. Cool in pan 5 minutes; loosen edges and remove rolls from pan.

4. For frosting, in small bowl, combine confectioners' sugar, remaining ⅓ cup EAGLE BRAND® and vanilla. Drizzle frosting over warm rolls. Sprinkle with additional chopped pecans (optional).   *Makes 12 rolls*

Mexican Monkey Bread

Prep Time: 15 minutes • **Stand Time:** 1 hour
Cook Time: 40 minutes

- **½ cup (1 stick) butter, melted**
- **2 tablespoons chili powder**
- **1 tablespoon ground cumin**
- **2 packages (about 16 ounces each) frozen bread dough, thawed and cut into 1-inch cubes**
- **2 cups (8 ounces) shredded Monterey Jack or Mexican blend cheese, divided**
- **2 cups _French's_® French Fried Onions, divided**
- **1 can (4½ ounces) chopped green chilies, drained**

1. Grease bottom and side of 10-inch tube pan. Combine melted butter and spices in small bowl. Dip bread cubes, one at a time, into butter mixture. Place ⅓ of bread cubes in bottom of prepared pan.

2. Sprinkle with ⅔ cup cheese, ⅔ _cup_ French Fried Onions and half of chilies. Repeat layers. Top with remaining ⅓ of bread cubes. Cover pan with plastic wrap* and place on baking sheet. Let rest in draft-free place for 1 hour or until doubled in size.

3. Preheat oven to 375°F. Bake 35 minutes or until golden. Sprinkle with remaining cheese and onions; bake 5 minutes or until cheese melts and onions are golden. Loosen edges of bread; invert onto baking rack. Immediately invert onto serving platter. Serve warm.

Makes 10 servings

Remove plastic wrap before baking.

Tomato-Artichoke Focaccia

1 package (16 ounces) hot roll mix
2 tablespoons wheat bran
1¼ cups hot water
4 teaspoons olive oil, divided
1 cup thinly sliced onions
2 cloves garlic, minced
4 ounces sun-dried tomatoes (not packed in oil),
  rehydrated* and cut into strips
1 cup canned artichoke hearts, cut into quarters
1 tablespoon minced fresh rosemary
2 tablespoons shredded Parmesan cheese

*To rehydrate sun-dried tomatoes, pour 1 cup boiling water over tomatoes in small heatproof bowl. Let tomatoes soak 5 to 10 minutes or until softened; drain well.

1. Preheat oven to 400°F. Spray 2 (9-inch) round cake pans with nonstick cooking spray.

2. Combine dry ingredients and contents of yeast packet from hot roll mix in large bowl. Add bran; mix well. Stir in hot water and 2 teaspoons oil. Knead dough about 5 minutes or until ingredients are blended. Press dough onto bottom of prepared pans. Cover and let rise 15 minutes.

3. Heat 1 teaspoon oil in medium skillet over low heat. Add onions and garlic; cook and stir 2 to 3 minutes or until onions are tender.

4. Brush surface of dough with remaining 1 teaspoon oil. Top dough with onion mixture, tomatoes, artichokes and rosemary. Sprinkle with Parmesan. Bake 25 to 30 minutes or until lightly browned on top.

Makes 16 servings

Blueberry White Chip Muffins

  2 cups all-purpose flour
  ½ cup granulated sugar
  ¼ cup packed brown sugar
  2½ teaspoons baking powder
  ½ teaspoon salt
  ¾ cup milk
  1 large egg, lightly beaten
  ¼ cup butter or margarine, melted
  ½ teaspoon grated lemon peel
  2 cups (12-ounce package) NESTLÉ® TOLL HOUSE® Premier White Morsels, *divided*
1½ cups fresh or frozen blueberries
  Streusel Topping (recipe follows)

PREHEAT oven to 375°F. Paper-line 18 muffin cups.

COMBINE flour, granulated sugar, brown sugar, baking powder and salt in large bowl. Stir in milk, egg, butter and lemon peel. Stir in *1½ cups* morsels and blueberries. Spoon into prepared muffin cups, filling almost full. Sprinkle with Streusel Topping.

BAKE for 22 to 25 minutes or until wooden pick inserted into centers comes out clean. Cool in pans for 5 minutes; remove to wire racks to cool slightly.

PLACE *remaining* morsels in small, *heavy-duty* resealable plastic food storage bag. Microwave on MEDIUM-HIGH (70%) power for 30 seconds; knead. Microwave at additional 10- to 15-second intervals, kneading until smooth. Cut tiny corner from bag; squeeze to drizzle over muffins. Serve warm.   *Makes 18 muffins*

Streusel Topping: COMBINE ⅓ cup granulated sugar, ¼ cup all-purpose flour and ¼ teaspoon ground cinnamon in small bowl. Cut in 3 tablespoons butter or margarine with pastry blender or two knives until mixture resembles coarse crumbs.

Apple Raisin Walnut Muffins

2 cups all-purpose flour
¾ cup sugar
2 teaspoons baking powder
1 teaspoon ground cinnamon
½ teaspoon baking soda
½ teaspoon salt
¼ teaspoon ground nutmeg
¾ cup plus 2 tablespoons milk
2 eggs, beaten
⅓ cup butter, melted
1 cup chopped dried apples
½ cup golden raisins
½ cup chopped walnuts

1. Preheat oven to 350°F. Grease 6 jumbo (3½-inch) muffin cups. Combine flour, sugar, baking powder, cinnamon, baking soda, salt and nutmeg in large bowl.

2. Beat together milk, eggs and butter in small bowl. Stir into flour mixture just until blended. Gently fold in apples, raisins and walnuts. Fill prepared muffin cups three-fourths full.

3. Bake 25 to 30 minutes or until toothpick inserted into centers comes out clean. Cool in pan 2 minutes; remove muffins to wire rack. Serve warm or at room temperature.   *Makes 6 jumbo muffins*

Honey Sweet Potato Biscuits

2 cups all-purpose flour
1 tablespoon baking powder
½ teaspoon salt
¼ cup vegetable shortening
1 tablespoon grated orange peel
1 tablespoon grated lemon peel
¾ cup mashed cooked sweet potato (1 large sweet potato baked until tender, peeled and mashed)
⅓ cup honey
½ cup milk (about)

Combine flour, baking powder and salt in large bowl. Cut in shortening until mixture is size of small peas. Add orange and lemon peels, sweet potato and honey; mix well. Add enough milk to make soft, but not sticky, dough. Knead 3 or 4 times on lightly floured surface. Pat dough to 1-inch thickness and cut into 2¼-inch rounds. Place on ungreased baking sheet.

Bake in preheated 400°F oven 15 to 18 minutes or until lightly browned. Serve warm.   *Makes 10 biscuits*

Favorite recipe from **National Honey Board**

Irish Soda Bread Rounds

4 cups all-purpose flour
¼ cup sugar
1 tablespoon baking powder
1 teaspoon baking soda
1 teaspoon salt
⅓ cup shortening
1 cup currants or raisins
1¾ cups buttermilk
1 egg

1. Preheat oven to 350°F. Grease 2 baking sheets; set aside.

2. Sift flour, sugar, baking powder, baking soda and salt into large bowl. Cut in shortening with pastry blender or 2 knives until mixture resembles coarse crumbs. Stir in currants.

3. Beat buttermilk and egg in medium bowl until well blended. Add buttermilk mixture to flour mixture; stir until mixture forms soft dough that clings together and forms a ball.

4. Turn out dough onto well-floured surface. Knead dough gently 10 to 12 times. Shape dough into 8 (3½-inch) rounds; place on prepared baking sheets. Score top of each round with tip of sharp knife, making an "X" about 1 inch long and ¼ inch deep.

5. Bake 25 to 28 minutes or until toothpick inserted into centers comes out clean. Immediately remove from baking sheets; cool on wire racks.

Makes 8 rounds

Note: For a sweet crust, combine 1 tablespoon sugar and 1 tablespoon water in small bowl; brush over hot bread.

*Tip

Irish soda bread is best eaten the same day it's made, so be sure to distribute these gift loaves soon after baking.

Potato Rosemary Rolls

Dough

        1 cup plus 2 tablespoons water (70° to 80°F)
        2 tablespoons olive oil
        1 teaspoon salt
        3 cups bread flour
        ½ cup instant potato flakes or buds
        2 tablespoons nonfat dry milk powder
        1 tablespoon sugar
        1 teaspoon SPICE ISLANDS® Rosemary, crushed
        1½ teaspoons FLEISCHMANN'S® Bread Machine Yeast

Topping

        1 egg, lightly beaten
            Sesame or poppy seeds or additional dried rosemary,
            crushed

Bread Machine Directions

Measure all dough ingredients into bread machine pan in the order suggested by manufacturer, adding potato flakes with flour. Select dough/manual cycle. When cycle is complete, remove dough to floured surface. If necessary, knead in additional flour to make dough easy to handle.

Divide dough into 12 equal pieces. Roll each piece to 10-inch rope; coil each rope and tuck end under coil. Place rolls 2 inches apart on large greased baking sheet. Cover; let rise in warm, draft-free place until doubled in size, about 45 to 60 minutes. Brush tops with beaten egg; sprinkle with sesame seeds. Bake at 375°F for 15 to 20 minutes or until done. Remove from pan; cool on wire rack.   *Makes 12 rolls*

Note: Dough can be prepared in 1½- and 2-pound bread machines.

Bacon Cheddar Muffins

2 cups all-purpose flour
¾ cup sugar
2 teaspoons baking powder
½ teaspoon baking soda
½ teaspoon salt
¾ cup plus 2 tablespoons milk
⅓ cup butter, melted
1 egg, lightly beaten
1 cup (4 ounces) shredded Cheddar cheese
½ cup crumbled crisp-cooked bacon (about 6 slices)

1. Preheat oven to 350°F. Grease 12 standard (2½-inch) muffin cups or line with paper baking cups.

2. Combine flour, sugar, baking powder, baking soda and salt in medium bowl. Combine milk, butter and egg in small bowl; mix well. Add milk mixture to flour mixture; stir just until blended. Gently stir in cheese and bacon. Spoon evenly into prepared muffin cups, filling three-fourths full.

3. Bake 15 to 20 minutes or until toothpick inserted into centers comes out clean. Cool muffins in pan 2 minutes; remove to wire rack. Serve warm or at room temperature. *Makes 12 muffins*

Lots o' Chocolate Bread

2 cups mini semisweet chocolate chips, divided
⅔ cup packed light brown sugar
½ cup (1 stick) butter, softened
2 eggs
2½ cups all-purpose flour
1½ cups applesauce
1½ teaspoons vanilla
1 teaspoon baking soda
1 teaspoon baking powder
½ teaspoon salt
1 tablespoon shortening (do not use butter, margarine, spread or oil)

1. Preheat oven to 350°F. Grease 5 mini (5½×3-inch) loaf pans. Place 1 cup chocolate chips in small microwavable bowl. Microwave on HIGH 1 minute; stir. Microwave at 30-second intervals, stirring after each interval, until chocolate is melted and smooth; set aside.

2. Beat brown sugar and butter in large bowl with electric mixer at medium speed until creamy. Add melted chocolate and eggs; beat until well blended. Add flour, applesauce, vanilla, baking soda, baking powder and salt; beat until well blended. Stir in ½ cup chocolate chips. Spoon batter evenly into prepared pans.

3. Bake 35 to 40 minutes or until centers crack and are dry to the touch. Cool in pans on wire racks 10 minutes. Remove from pans; cool completely.

4. Place remaining ½ cup chocolate chips and shortening in small microwavable bowl. Microwave on HIGH 1 minute; stir. Microwave at 30-second intervals, stirring after each interval, until chocolate is melted and mixture is smooth. Drizzle glaze over loaves; let stand until set.

Makes 5 mini loaves

Gift Idea: Wrap each loaf in plastic wrap or cellophane and place in a colorful gift bag. With each loaf include a sampling of single serving packets of gourmet coffee or tea.

Tangy Lime Bars
(p. 48)

Mocha Brownie Cookies
(p. 40)

Caribbean Crunch
Shortbread (p. 52)

Mississippi Mud Bars
(p. 36)

Cookies & Bars

Snickerdoodles

¾ cup plus 1 tablespoon sugar, divided
2 teaspoons cinnamon, divided
1⅓ cups all-purpose flour
1 teaspoon cream of tartar
½ teaspoon baking soda
½ cup (1 stick) butter
1 egg
1 cup (6 ounces) cinnamon baking chips
1 cup raisins (optional)

1. Preheat oven to 400°F. Combine 1 tablespoon sugar and 1 teaspoon cinnamon in small bowl; set aside.

2. Combine flour, remaining 1 teaspoon cinnamon, cream of tartar and baking soda in medium bowl. Beat remaining ¾ cup sugar and butter in large bowl with electric mixer at medium speed until creamy. Beat in egg. Gradually add flour mixture to sugar mixture, beating at low speed until stiff dough forms. Stir in cinnamon chips and raisins, if desired.

3. Roll tablespoonfuls of dough into 1-inch balls; roll balls in reserved cinnamon-sugar. Place on ungreased cookie sheets.

4. Bake 10 minutes or until firm in center. *Do not overbake.* Remove to wire racks; cool completely.   *Makes about 3 dozen cookies*

Almond Fudge Topped Shortbread

1 cup (2 sticks) butter or margarine, softened
½ cup powdered sugar
¼ teaspoon salt
1¼ cups all-purpose flour
2 cups (12-ounce package) HERSHEY'S Semi-Sweet Chocolate Chips
1 (14-ounce) can sweetened condensed milk (not evaporated milk)
½ teaspoon almond extract
½ cup sliced almonds, toasted

1. Heat oven to 350°F. Grease 13×9×2-inch baking pan.

2. Beat butter, powdered sugar and salt in large bowl until fluffy. Add flour; mix well. With floured hands, press evenly into prepared pan.

3. Bake 20 minutes or until lightly browned.

4. Melt chocolate chips and sweetened condensed milk in heavy saucepan over low heat, stirring constantly. Remove from heat; stir in extract. Spread evenly over baked shortbread. Garnish with almonds; press down firmly. Cool. Chill 3 hours or until firm. Cut into bars. Store covered at room temperature. *Makes 24 to 36 bars*

Toffee Chipsters

1 package (18 ounces) refrigerated sugar cookie dough
1 cup white chocolate chips
1 bag (8 ounces) chocolate-covered toffee baking bits, divided

1. Preheat oven to 350°F. Lightly grease cookie sheets. Let dough stand at room temperature about 15 minutes.

2. Beat dough, white chocolate chips and 1 cup toffee bits in large bowl with electric mixer at medium speed until well blended. Drop dough by rounded tablespoonfuls 2 inches apart onto prepared cookie sheets. Press remaining ⅓ cup toffee bits into dough mounds.

3. Bake 10 to 12 minutes or until set. Cool on cookie sheets 1 minute. Remove to wire racks; cool completely.   *Makes about 2 dozen cookies*

Mississippi Mud Bars

¾ cup packed brown sugar
½ cup (1 stick) butter, softened
1 egg
1 teaspoon vanilla
½ teaspoon baking soda
¼ teaspoon salt
1 cup plus 2 tablespoons all-purpose flour
1 cup (6 ounces) semisweet chocolate chips, divided
1 cup (6 ounces) white chocolate chips, divided
½ cup chopped walnuts or pecans

1. Preheat oven to 375°F. Line 9-inch square pan with foil; grease foil.

2. Beat sugar and butter in large bowl with electric mixer at medium speed until creamy. Beat in egg and vanilla until light and fluffy. Blend in baking soda and salt. Add flour, mixing until well blended. Stir in ⅔ cup semisweet chips, ⅔ cup white chocolate chips and nuts. Spread dough in prepared pan.

3. Bake 23 to 25 minutes or until center feels firm. *Do not overbake.* Remove from oven; sprinkle with remaining ⅓ cup semisweet chips and ⅓ cup white chocolate chips. Let stand until chips melt; spread evenly over bars. Cool in pan on wire rack until chocolate is set. Cut into bars or triangles. *Makes about 3 dozen bars or triangles*

Malted Milk Cookies

  1 cup (2 sticks) butter, softened
  ¾ cup granulated sugar
  ¾ cup packed light brown sugar
  1 teaspoon baking soda
  2 eggs
  2 squares (1 ounce each) unsweetened chocolate, melted
     and cooled to room temperature
  1 teaspoon vanilla
 2¼ cups all-purpose flour
  ½ cup malted milk powder
  1 cup chopped malted milk balls

1. Preheat oven to 375°F.

2. Beat butter in large bowl with electric mixer at medium speed
30 seconds. Add granulated sugar, brown sugar and baking soda; beat
until blended. Add eggs, chocolate and vanilla; beat until well blended.

3. Beat in as much flour as possible with mixer. Using spoon, stir in any
remaining flour and malted milk powder. Stir in malted milk balls.

4. Drop dough by rounded tablespoonfuls 2½ inches apart onto
ungreased cookie sheets. Bake about 10 minutes or until edges are firm.
Cool on cookie sheets 1 minute. Remove to wire racks; cool completely.

Makes about 3 dozen cookies

Peanut Butter Cookie Bars

1 package (18 ounces) refrigerated peanut butter cookie dough
1 can (14 ounces) sweetened condensed milk
¼ cup all-purpose flour
¼ cup peanut butter
1 cup peanut butter chips
1 cup chopped peanuts

1. Preheat oven to 350°F. Lightly grease 13×9-inch baking pan. Let dough stand at room temperature about 15 minutes.

2. Press dough evenly onto bottom of prepared pan. Bake 10 minutes.

3. Meanwhile, combine sweetened condensed milk, flour and peanut butter in medium bowl; beat with electric mixer at medium speed until well blended. Spoon over partially baked crust. Sprinkle evenly with peanut butter chips and peanuts; press down lightly.

4. Bake 15 to 18 minutes or until center is set. Cool completely in pan on wire rack.   *Makes about 2 dozen bars*

Mocha Brownie Cookies

1 cup granulated sugar
¾ cup packed brown sugar
½ cup (1 stick) butter, softened
¼ cup sour cream
1 tablespoon instant coffee, dissolved in 2 tablespoons cooled brewed coffee
2 eggs
2½ cups all-purpose flour
⅓ cup unsweetened cocoa powder
1 teaspoon baking soda
1 teaspoon baking powder
1 teaspoon salt
1½ cups semisweet chocolate chips

1. Preheat oven to 325°F.

2. Beat sugars, butter, sour cream and coffee mixture in large bowl with electric mixer at medium speed until creamy. Add eggs one at a time, beating well after each addition.

3. Combine flour, cocoa, baking soda, baking powder and salt in medium bowl. Gradually add to butter mixture, beating at low speed just until blended. Beat 1 minute at medium speed until dough is well blended. Stir in chocolate chips.

4. Drop dough by rounded tablespoonfuls onto ungreased cookie sheets. Bake 9 to 11 minutes or until slight imprint remains when pressed with finger. Cool 3 minutes on cookie sheets. Remove to wire racks; cool completely.   *Makes 5 to 6 dozen cookies*

Cocoa Bottom
Banana Pecan Bars

      1 cup sugar
      ½ cup (1 stick) butter, softened
      5 ripe bananas, mashed
      1 egg
      1 teaspoon vanilla
   1½ cups all-purpose flour
      1 teaspoon baking powder
      1 teaspoon baking soda
      ½ teaspoon salt
      ½ cup chopped pecans
      ¼ cup unsweetened cocoa powder

1. Preheat oven to 350°F. Grease 13×9-inch baking pan; set aside.

2. Beat sugar and butter in large bowl with electric mixer at medium speed until creamy. Add bananas, egg and vanilla; beat until well blended. Combine flour, baking powder, baking soda and salt in medium bowl. Add to banana mixture; beat until well blended. Stir in pecans.

3. Divide batter in half. Stir cocoa into one half. Spread cocoa batter in prepared pan. Spread plain batter over cocoa batter; swirl with knife.

4. Bake 30 to 35 minutes or until edges are lightly browned and toothpick inserted into center comes out clean. Cool completely in pan on wire rack. Cut into squares.   *Makes 15 to 18 squares*

Colorful Cookie Buttons

1½ cups (3 sticks) butter, softened
½ cup granulated sugar
½ cup firmly packed light brown sugar
2 large egg yolks
1 teaspoon vanilla extract
3½ cups all-purpose flour
1½ teaspoons baking powder
½ teaspoon salt
1 cup "M&M's"® Chocolate Mini Baking Bits

Preheat oven to 350°F. In large bowl cream butter and sugars until light and fluffy; beat in egg yolks and vanilla. In medium bowl combine flour, baking powder and salt; add to creamed mixture. Shape dough into 72 balls. For each cookie, place one ball on ungreased cookie sheet and flatten. Place 8 to 10 "M&M's"® Chocolate Mini Baking Bits on dough. Flatten second ball and place over "M&M's"® Chocolate Mini Baking Bits, pressing top and bottom dough together. Decorate top with remaining "M&M's"® Chocolate Mini Baking Bits. Repeat with remaining dough balls and "M&M's"® Chocolate Mini Baking Bits, placing cookies about 2 inches apart on cookie sheets. Bake 17 to 18 minutes. Cool 2 minutes on cookie sheets; cool completely on wire racks. Store in tightly covered container.

Makes 3 dozen cookies

Toffee-Top
Cheesecake Bars

Prep Time: 20 minutes • **Bake Time:** 40 minutes
Cool Time: 15 minutes

1¼ **cups all-purpose flour**
1 **cup confectioners' sugar**
½ **cup unsweetened cocoa**
¼ **teaspoon baking soda**
¾ **cup (1½ sticks) butter or margarine**
1 **(8-ounce) package cream cheese, softened**
1 **(14-ounce) can EAGLE BRAND® Sweetened Condensed Milk (NOT evaporated milk)**
2 **eggs**
1 **teaspoon vanilla extract**
1½ **cups (8-ounce package) English toffee bits, divided**

1. Preheat oven to 350°F. In medium bowl, combine flour, confectioners' sugar, cocoa and baking soda; cut in butter until mixture is crumbly. Press firmly on bottom of ungreased 13×9-inch baking pan. Bake 15 minutes.

2. In large bowl, beat cream cheese until fluffy. Add EAGLE BRAND®, eggs and vanilla; beat until smooth. Stir in 1 cup English toffee bits. Pour mixture over hot crust. Bake 25 minutes or until set and edges just begin to brown.

3. Cool 15 minutes. Sprinkle remaining ½ cup English toffee bits evenly over top. Cool completely. Refrigerate several hours or until cold. Store leftovers covered in refrigerator.   *Makes about 3 dozen bars*

Apple Cinnamon Chunkies

1 package (18 ounces) refrigerated oatmeal raisin cookie dough
1 cup chopped dried apples
½ cup cinnamon baking chips
½ teaspoon apple pie spice*

*You may substitute ¼ teaspoon ground cinnamon, ⅛ teaspoon ground nutmeg and pinch of ground allspice or ground cloves for ½ teaspoon apple pie spice.

1. Preheat oven to 350°F. Lightly grease cookie sheets. Let dough stand at room temperature about 15 minutes.

2. Combine dough, apples, cinnamon chips and apple pie spice in large bowl; stir until well blended. Drop dough by rounded tablespoonfuls 2 inches apart onto prepared cookie sheets.

3. Bake 10 to 12 minutes or until golden brown. Cool on cookie sheets 2 to 3 minutes. Remove to wire racks; cool completely.

Makes 2 dozen cookies

Chocolate Chip Macaroons

2½ cups flaked coconut
⅔ cup mini semisweet chocolate chips
⅔ cup sweetened condensed milk
1 teaspoon vanilla

1. Preheat oven to 350°F. Grease cookie sheets. Combine coconut, chocolate chips, milk and vanilla in medium bowl; mix until well blended.

2. Drop dough by rounded teaspoonfuls 2 inches apart onto prepared cookie sheets. Press dough gently with back of spoon to flatten slightly. Bake 10 to 12 minutes or until light golden brown. Let cookies stand on cookie sheets 1 minute. Remove cookies to wire racks; cool completely.

Makes about 3½ dozen cookies

Chocolate Dream Bars

2¼ cups all-purpose flour, divided
1 cup (2 sticks) butter, softened
¾ cup powdered sugar
⅓ cup unsweetened cocoa powder
2 cups granulated sugar
4 eggs, beaten
4 squares (1 ounce each) unsweetened baking chocolate, melted
Additional powdered sugar (optional)

1. Preheat oven to 350°F.

2. Combine 2 cups flour, butter, ¾ cup powdered sugar and cocoa in large bowl; beat until well blended and stiff dough forms. Press firmly into ungreased 13×9-inch baking pan. Bake 15 to 20 minutes or just until set. *Do not overbake.*

3. Meanwhile, combine remaining ¼ cup flour and granulated sugar in medium bowl. Stir in eggs and melted chocolate; beat until blended. Pour over crust.

4. Bake 25 minutes or until toothpick inserted into center comes out clean. Cool completely in pan on wire rack. Sprinkle with powdered sugar, if desired. Cut into bars.   *Makes 3 dozen bars*

*Tip

Add a decorative touch to these bars with a powdered sugar design. Place a stencil, doily or strips of paper on top of the bars, then dust lightly with powdered sugar. Carefully lift the stencil straight up, holding it firmly by the edges.

Lemony Butter Cookies

½ **cup (1 stick) butter, softened**
½ **cup sugar**
1 **egg**
1½ **cups all-purpose flour**
2 **tablespoons fresh lemon juice**
1 **teaspoon grated lemon peel**
½ **teaspoon baking powder**
⅛ **teaspoon salt**
   Additional sugar

1. Beat butter and sugar in large bowl with electric mixer at medium speed until creamy. Beat in egg until light and fluffy. Mix in flour, lemon juice, lemon peel, baking powder and salt. Wrap in plastic wrap; refrigerate about 2 hours or until firm.

2. Preheat oven to 350°F. Roll out dough, a small portion at a time, on well-floured surface to ¼-inch thickness. (Keep remaining dough in refrigerator.) Cut dough with 3-inch round or fluted cookie cutter. Transfer cutouts to ungreased cookie sheets. Sprinkle with sugar.

3. Bake 8 to 10 minutes or until edges are lightly browned. Cool 1 minute on cookie sheets. Remove to wire racks; cool completely. Store in airtight container. *Makes about 2½ dozen cookies*

Tangy Lime Bars

1 package (18 ounces) refrigerated sugar cookie dough
¾ cup all-purpose flour, divided
1¼ cups granulated sugar
4 eggs
½ cup bottled key lime juice
1 drop green food coloring
1 teaspoon baking powder
Powdered sugar

1. Preheat oven to 350°F. Lightly grease 13×9-inch baking pan. Let dough stand at room temperature about 15 minutes.

2. Beat dough and ½ cup flour in large bowl with electric mixer at medium speed until well blended. Press dough evenly onto bottom and ½ inch up sides of prepared pan. Bake 20 minutes.

3. Meanwhile, combine granulated sugar, eggs, lime juice and food coloring in large bowl; beat at medium speed until well blended. Add remaining ¼ cup flour and baking powder; beat until well blended. Pour over baked crust.

4. Bake 18 to 21 minutes or until edges are brown and center is just set. Cool completely in pan on wire rack. Sprinkle with powdered sugar just before serving. Store covered in refrigerator.   *Makes 2 dozen bars*

Chunky Chocolate Chip Peanut Butter Cookies

1 ¼ cups all-purpose flour
½ teaspoon baking soda
½ teaspoon salt
½ teaspoon ground cinnamon
¾ cup (1 ½ sticks) butter or margarine, softened
½ cup granulated sugar
½ cup packed brown sugar
½ cup creamy peanut butter
1 large egg
1 teaspoon vanilla extract
2 cups (12-ounce package) NESTLÉ® TOLL HOUSE® Semi-Sweet Chocolate Morsels
½ cup coarsely chopped peanuts

PREHEAT oven to 375°F.

COMBINE flour, baking soda, salt and cinnamon in small bowl. Beat butter, granulated sugar, brown sugar and peanut butter in large mixer bowl until creamy. Beat in egg and vanilla extract. Gradually beat in flour mixture. Stir in morsels and peanuts.

DROP dough by rounded tablespoon onto ungreased baking sheets. Press down slightly to flatten into 2-inch circles.

BAKE for 7 to 10 minutes or until edges are set but centers are still soft. Cool on baking sheets for 4 minutes; remove to wire racks to cool completely.   *Makes about 3 dozen cookies*

Piña Colada Cookie Bars

½ cup (1 stick) butter, melted
1½ cups graham cracker crumbs
1 can (14 ounces) sweetened condensed milk
2 tablespoons dark rum
2 cups white chocolate chips
1 cup flaked coconut
½ cup chopped macadamia nuts
½ cup chopped dried pineapple

1. Preheat oven to 350°F.

2. Pour butter into 13×9-inch baking pan, tilting pan to coat bottom. Sprinkle crumbs evenly over butter. Combine sweetened condensed milk and rum in small bowl; pour over crumbs. Top with white chips, coconut, nuts and pineapple.

3. Bake 25 to 30 minutes or until edges are lightly browned. Cut into bars with serrated knife. Store loosely covered at room temperature.

Makes 3 dozen bars

Caribbean Crunch
Shortbread

1 cup (2 sticks) unsalted butter, softened
½ cup powdered sugar
2 tablespoons firmly packed light brown sugar
¼ teaspoon salt
2 cups all-purpose flour
1 cup diced dried tropical fruit mix (such as pineapple,
**   mango and papaya)**

1. Beat butter, sugars and salt in large bowl with electric mixer at medium speed until creamy. Add flour, ½ cup at a time, beating after each addition. Stir in tropical fruit.

2. Shape dough into 14-inch log. Wrap in plastic wrap; refrigerate 1 hour.

3. Preheat oven to 300°F. Cut log into ½-inch-thick slices; place on ungreased cookie sheets. Bake 20 to 25 minutes or until cookies are set and lightly browned. Cool 5 minutes on cookie sheets; transfer to wire racks to cool completely. *Makes 28 cookies*

*Tip

Use decorative cookie tins, baskets or practical baking pans for packaging all of your best home-baked cookies and bars, and you'll be giving a gift that lasts long after the cookies are gone. Be sure to pack the cookies snugly to prevent them from breaking. Try using colorful new dish towels or decorative cloth napkins to cushion the cookies—yet another unexpected gift!

Peanut Butter Truffles
(p. 59)

Toll House® Famous Fudge
(p. 60)

White Truffles
(p. 74)

Pecan Candy
(p. 67)

Candy & Treats

Coconut Bonbons

2 cups powdered sugar
1 cup flaked coconut
3 tablespoons evaporated milk
2 tablespoons butter, softened
1 teaspoon vanilla
1 cup (6 ounces) semisweet chocolate chips
1 tablespoon shortening
   Toasted coconut* and/or melted white chocolate (optional)

*To toast coconut, spread evenly on baking sheet. Toast in preheated 350°F oven 5 to 7 minutes, stirring occasionally, until light golden brown.

1. Line baking sheet with waxed paper; set aside.

2. Combine powdered sugar, coconut, milk, butter and vanilla in medium bowl. Stir until well blended. Shape mixture into 1-inch balls; place on prepared baking sheet. Refrigerate until firm.

3. Combine chocolate chips and shortening in small microwavable bowl. Microwave on HIGH 1 minute; stir. Microwave at 30-second intervals, stirring after each interval, until chocolate is melted and mixture is smooth.

4. Dip bonbons in melted chocolate using toothpick or wooden skewer. Remove excess chocolate by scraping bottom of bonbon across bowl rim; return to prepared baking sheet. Sprinkle some bonbons with toasted coconut, if desired. Refrigerate all bonbons until firm. Drizzle plain bonbons with melted white chocolate, if desired. Store in refrigerator.

Makes about 3 dozen bonbons

*Tip

Place the bonbons in petits fours or paper candy cups. Arrange some crinkled paper gift basket filler in the bottom of a tin or gift box and nestle the candies in the filler. Or, for party favors or small gifts, place 3 or 4 bonbons in a cellophane bag and tie it with 2 pieces of different colored curling ribbon.

Yuletide Twisters

1 package (6 ounces) premier white baking bars
1 tablespoon plus 1 teaspoon milk
1 tablespoon plus 1 teaspoon light corn syrup
8 ounces reduced-salt pretzel twists (about 80)
   Chocolate sprinkles, cookie decorations, colored sugars

1. Line baking sheet with waxed paper; set aside.

2. Melt baking bars in small saucepan over low heat, stirring constantly. Stir in milk and corn syrup. Do not remove saucepan from heat.

3. Holding pretzel with fork, dip 1 side of pretzel into melted mixture to coat. Place coated side up on prepared baking sheet; immediately sprinkle with desired decorations. Repeat with remaining pretzels. Refrigerate 15 to 20 minutes or until firm.   *Makes 10 servings*

Chocolate Twisters: Substitute 1 cup semisweet chocolate chips for white baking bars.

Caramel Dippity Do's: Heat 1 cup caramel sauce and ⅓ cup finely chopped pecans in small saucepan over low heat until warm. Pour into small serving bowl. Serve with pretzels for dipping. Makes 8 servings.

Chocolate Dippity Do's: Heat 1 cup hot fudge sauce and ⅓ cup finely chopped pecans or walnuts in small saucepan over low heat until warm. Pour into small serving bowl. Serve with pretzels for dipping. Makes 8 servings.

Peanut Butter Truffles

2 cups (11½ ounces) milk chocolate chips
½ cup whipping cream
2 tablespoons butter
½ cup creamy peanut butter
¾ cup finely chopped peanuts

1. Heat chocolate chips, whipping cream and butter in medium heavy saucepan over low heat, stirring occasionally. Add peanut butter; stir until smooth and blended. Pour into pie pan. Refrigerate about 1 hour or until mixture is fudgy but soft, stirring occasionally.

2. Shape mixture by tablespoonfuls into 1¼-inch balls; place on waxed paper. Place peanuts in shallow bowl. Roll balls in peanuts; place in petits fours or paper candy cups. (If peanuts won't stick because truffle has set, roll truffle between palms until outside is soft.) Truffles can be refrigerated 2 to 3 days or frozen several weeks. *Makes about 3 dozen truffles*

Variation: Roll some of the truffles in cocoa powder instead of chopped peanuts.

Toll House®
Famous Fudge

1½ cups granulated sugar
⅔ cup (5 fluid-ounce can) NESTLÉ® CARNATION® Evaporated Milk
2 tablespoons butter or margarine
¼ teaspoon salt
2 cups miniature marshmallows
1½ cups (9 ounces) NESTLÉ® TOLL HOUSE® Semi-Sweet Chocolate Morsels
½ cup chopped pecans or walnuts (optional)
1 teaspoon vanilla extract

LINE 8-inch square baking pan with foil.

COMBINE sugar, evaporated milk, butter and salt in medium, *heavy-duty* saucepan. Bring to a *full rolling boil* over medium heat, stirring constantly. Boil, stirring constantly, for 4 to 5 minutes. Remove from heat.

STIR in marshmallows, morsels, nuts and vanilla extract. Stir vigorously for 1 minute or until marshmallows are melted. Pour into prepared baking pan; refrigerate for 2 hours or until firm. Lift from pan; remove foil. Cut into pieces. *Makes 49 pieces*

For Milk Chocolate Fudge: SUBSTITUTE 1¾ cups (11.5-ounce package) NESTLÉ® TOLL HOUSE® Milk Chocolate Morsels for Semi-Sweet Morsels.

For Butterscotch Fudge: SUBSTITUTE 1⅔ cups (11-ounce package) NESTLÉ® TOLL HOUSE® Butterscotch Flavored Morsels for Semi-Sweet Morsels.

For Peanutty Chocolate Fudge: SUBSTITUTE 1⅔ cups (11-ounce package) NESTLÉ® TOLL HOUSE® Peanut Butter & Milk Chocolate Morsels for Semi-Sweet Morsels and ½ cup chopped peanuts for pecans or walnuts.

Maple-Cashew Brittle

1 cup sugar
1 cup maple-flavored syrup*
¼ cup water
3 tablespoons butter
1½ cups lightly salted roasted cashews
¼ teaspoon baking soda

*Do not use pure maple syrup.

1. Lightly butter 15×10×1-inch jelly-roll pan.

2. Combine sugar, syrup, water and butter in medium heavy saucepan. Bring to a boil over medium heat, stirring occasionally. Attach candy thermometer to side of pan, making sure bulb is submerged in sugar mixture but not touching bottom of pan. Continue boiling, without stirring, about 25 minutes or until mixture reaches hard-crack stage (300° to 305°F) on candy thermometer. (Watch carefully, making sure mixture does not burn.) Remove from heat; immediately stir in cashews and baking soda.

3. Immediately pour into prepared pan, quickly spreading to edges of pan and making sure cashews are spread in single layer. Cool completely, about 30 minutes. Break into pieces. Store in airtight container at room temperature up to 4 weeks.   *Makes about 1¼ pounds brittle*

Traditional Nut Brittle: Substitute light corn syrup for maple-flavored syrup and deluxe mixed nuts without peanuts for cashews. Proceed as directed.

Buttery Peppermints

20 hard peppermint candies
5½ cups powdered sugar, divided
⅓ cup evaporated milk
¼ cup (½ stick) butter

1. Place peppermint candies and ½ cup powdered sugar in food processor; process using on/off pulsing action until consistency of powder.

2. Cook and stir evaporated milk, butter and ½ cup powdered candy mixture in large heavy saucepan over medium-low heat until candy dissolves and mixture just begins to boil. Transfer to large bowl.

3. Stir 4 cups powdered sugar into milk mixture until well blended. Stir in additional powdered sugar, ¼ cup at a time, until consistency of dough.

4. Place dough on surface lightly dusted with powdered sugar. Knead until smooth. Divide into 4 equal portions.

5. Shape each portion into 20-inch-long roll. Cut each roll into ¾-inch pieces. Roll in remaining powdered candy mixture to coat.

6. For soft mints, store in airtight container at room temperature. For dry mints, keep uncovered several hours before storing in airtight container.

Makes about 8 dozen mints

Chocolate Mint Truffles

1¾ cups (11.5-ounce package) NESTLÉ® TOLL HOUSE® Milk Chocolate Morsels
1 cup (6 ounces) NESTLÉ® TOLL HOUSE® Semi-Sweet Chocolate Morsels
¾ cup heavy whipping cream
1 tablespoon peppermint extract
1½ cups finely chopped walnuts, toasted, or NESTLÉ® TOLL HOUSE® Baking Cocoa

LINE baking sheet with waxed paper.

PLACE milk chocolate and semi-sweet morsels in large mixer bowl. Heat cream to a gentle boil in small saucepan; pour over morsels. Let stand for 1 minute; stir until smooth. Stir in peppermint extract. Cover with plastic wrap; refrigerate for 35 to 45 minutes or until slightly thickened. Stir just until color lightens slightly. (*Do not* overmix or truffles will be grainy.)

DROP by rounded teaspoon onto prepared baking sheet; refrigerate for 10 to 15 minutes. Shape into balls; roll in walnuts or cocoa. Store in airtight container in refrigerator.   *Makes about 48 truffles*

Variation: After rolling chocolate mixture into balls, freeze for 30 to 40 minutes. Microwave 1¾ cups (11.5-ounce package) NESTLÉ® TOLL HOUSE® Milk Chocolate Morsels and 3 tablespoons vegetable shortening in medium, uncovered, microwave-safe bowl on MEDIUM-HIGH (70%) power for 1 minute. STIR. Morsels may retain some of their original shape. If necessary, microwave at additional 10- to 15-second intervals, stirring just until morsels are melted. Dip truffles into chocolate mixture; shake off excess. Place on foil-lined baking sheets. Refrigerate for 15 to 20 minutes or until set. Store in airtight container in refrigerator.

Festive Caramel Apples

5 wooden popsicle sticks
5 medium apples
¾ cup chopped walnuts or pecans
1 package (14 ounces) caramels, unwrapped
1 tablespoon water
1 cup (6 ounces) semisweet chocolate chips
1 teaspoon shortening

1. Spray baking sheet with nonstick cooking spray; set aside. Insert wooden sticks into stem ends of apples. Place nuts in shallow dish.

2. Combine caramels and water in small saucepan. Cook over medium heat, stirring constantly, until caramels are melted.

3. Dip apples, one at a time, into caramel mixture, turning to cover completely. Remove excess caramel mixture by scraping apple bottoms across rim of saucepan.

4. Roll bottom halves of apples in walnuts. Place on prepared baking sheet. Refrigerate at least 15 minutes.

5. Place chocolate chips and shortening in small microwavable bowl. Microwave on HIGH 1 to 2 minutes; stir until chips are melted. Drizzle chocolate decoratively over apples. Refrigerate 10 minutes or until chocolate is firm.

6. Wrap apples individually; store in refrigerator.   *Makes 5 apples*

Pecan Candy

2 cups sugar
½ cup water
2 teaspoons ground cinnamon
¼ teaspoon ground allspice
⅛ teaspoon ground nutmeg
1 teaspoon red food coloring
1 teaspoon vanilla
4 cups (16 ounces) pecans

1. Line baking sheet with foil and lightly grease; set aside. Attach candy thermometer to side of medium saucepan; do not let bulb touch bottom of pan. Add sugar and water; bring to a boil over medium-high heat, stirring constantly. *Reduce heat to medium.*

2. Combine cinnamon, allspice and nutmeg in small bowl. Add spice mixture and food coloring to sugar mixture; mix well. Continue heating, stirring constantly, until mixture reaches 240°F (soft ball stage), about 5 minutes.

3. Add vanilla and pecans. Immediately pour pecan mixture onto prepared pan; cool 5 minutes. Pull pecans apart in individual pieces. Cool completely.   *Makes about 1 pound candy*

Fruit Bars

1 cup chopped dried figs
1 cup chopped dates
1 cup chopped dried pears
1 cup finely chopped pecans
¼ cup orange marmalade

1. Grease 8-inch square pan; set aside.

2. Combine all ingredients in medium bowl. Press mixture into prepared pan. Refrigerate until set.

3. Cut into bars. Store in refrigerator.   *Makes 32 bars*

Peanut Butter
Chip Tassies

1 package (3 ounces) cream cheese, softened
½ cup (1 stick) butter, softened
1 cup all-purpose flour
½ cup sugar
1 egg, slightly beaten
2 tablespoons butter, melted
¼ teaspoon lemon juice
¼ teaspoon vanilla extract
1 cup REESE'S® Peanut Butter Chips, chopped*
6 red candied cherries, quartered (optional)

Do not chop peanut butter chips in food processor or blender.

1. Beat cream cheese and ½ cup butter in medium bowl; stir in flour. Cover; refrigerate about one hour or until dough is firm. Shape into 24 one-inch balls; place each ball in ungreased small muffin cup (1¾ inches in diameter). Press dough evenly against bottom and side of each cup.

2. Heat oven to 350°F.

3. Combine sugar, egg, melted butter, lemon juice and vanilla in medium bowl; stir until smooth. Add chopped peanut butter chips. Fill muffin cups ¾ full with mixture.

4. Bake 20 to 25 minutes or until filling is set and lightly browned. Cool completely; remove from pan to wire rack. Garnish with candied cherries, if desired. *Makes about 2 dozen*

Peppermint Chocolate Fudge

Prep Time: 10 minutes • **Chill Time:** 2 hours

2 cups (12 ounces) milk chocolate chips
1 cup (6 ounces) semi-sweet chocolate chips
1 (14-ounce) can EAGLE BRAND® Sweetened Condensed Milk
    (NOT evaporated milk)
Dash salt
½ teaspoon peppermint extract
¼ cup crushed hard peppermint candy

1. In heavy saucepan over low heat, melt chocolate chips with EAGLE BRAND® and salt. Remove from heat; stir in peppermint extract. Spread evenly in wax-paper-lined 8- or 9-inch square pan. Sprinkle with peppermint candy.

2. Chill 2 hours or until firm. Turn fudge onto cutting board; peel off paper and cut into squares. Store leftovers covered in refrigerator.

Makes about 2 pounds fudge

Cranberry Gorp

¼ cup (½ stick) butter
¼ cup packed light brown sugar
1 tablespoon maple syrup
1 teaspoon curry powder
½ teaspoon ground cinnamon
1½ cups dried cranberries
1½ cups coarsely chopped walnuts and/or slivered almonds
1½ cups lightly salted pretzel nuggets

1. Preheat oven to 300°F. Grease 15×10-inch jelly-roll pan. Combine butter, brown sugar and maple syrup in large saucepan; heat over medium heat until butter is melted. Stir in curry powder and cinnamon. Add cranberries, walnuts and pretzels; stir until well blended.

2. Spread mixture on prepared pan. Bake 15 minutes or until mixture is lightly browned.

Makes 20 servings

Creamy
Caramels

½ cup slivered or chopped toasted almonds (optional)
1 cup (2 sticks) butter or margarine, cut into small pieces
2 cups sugar
1 can (14 ounces) sweetened condensed milk
1 cup light corn syrup
1½ teaspoons vanilla

1. Line 8-inch square baking pan with foil, extending edges over sides of pan. Lightly grease foil; sprinkle almonds onto bottom of pan, if desired.

2. Melt butter in medium heavy saucepan over low heat. Add sugar, sweetened condensed milk and corn syrup. Stir over low heat until sugar is dissolved and mixture comes to a boil.

3. Carefully clip candy thermometer to side of pan. (Do not let bulb touch bottom of pan.) Cook over low heat about 30 minutes or until thermometer registers 240°F (soft-ball stage), stirring occasionally. Immediately remove from heat and stir in vanilla. Pour mixture into prepared pan. Cool completely.

4. Using foil, lift caramels out of pan; remove foil. Place caramels on cutting board; cut into 1-inch squares with sharp knife. Wrap each square in plastic wrap. Store in airtight container.

Makes about 2½ pounds (64 caramels)

Marbled Caramels: Before cooling, add ⅓ cup chocolate chips to top. Let soften; swirl lightly into caramel using a knife.

Cashew & Pretzel Toffee Clusters

¾ cup packed brown sugar
¾ cup light corn syrup
½ cup (1 stick) butter
2 teaspoons vanilla
4 cups tiny pretzel twists (not sticks)
4 cups bite-size toasted wheat cereal squares
1 can (10 ounces) salted cashew halves and pieces

1. Preheat oven to 300°F. Spray large baking sheet with nonstick cooking spray; set aside.

2. Place brown sugar, corn syrup and butter in small heavy saucepan. Heat over medium heat until mixture boils and sugar dissolves, stirring frequently. Remove from heat; stir in vanilla.

3. Combine pretzels, cereal and cashews in large bowl. Pour sugar mixture over pretzel mixture; toss to coat evenly. Spread onto prepared baking sheet. Bake 30 minutes, stirring after 15 minutes. Spread onto greased waxed paper. Cool completely; break into clusters. Store in airtight container at room temperature. *Makes about 8 cups clusters*

White
Truffles

2 pounds vanilla-flavored candy coating*
**1 (14-ounce) can EAGLE BRAND® Sweetened Condensed Milk
(NOT evaporated milk)**
1 tablespoon vanilla extract
**1 pound chocolate-flavored candy coating,* melted, or
unsweetened cocoa**

*Also called confectionery coating or almond bark. If it is not available in your local
supermarket, it can be purchased in candy specialty stores.*

1. In heavy saucepan, over low heat, melt vanilla candy coating with
EAGLE BRAND®. Remove from heat; stir in vanilla. Cool.

2. Shape into 1-inch balls. With toothpick, partially dip each ball into
melted chocolate candy coating or roll in cocoa. Place on wax-paper-lined
baking sheets until firm. Store leftovers covered in refrigerator.

Makes about 8 dozen truffles

Flavoring Options: Amaretto: Omit vanilla. Add 3 tablespoons
amaretto or other almond-flavored liqueur and ½ teaspoon almond
extract. Roll in finely chopped toasted almonds. **Orange:** Omit vanilla.
Add 3 tablespoons orange-flavored liqueur. Roll in finely chopped toasted
almonds mixed with finely grated orange peel. **Rum:** Omit vanilla. Add
¼ cup dark rum. Roll in flaked coconut. **Bourbon:** Omit vanilla. Add
3 tablespoons bourbon. Roll in finely chopped toasted nuts.

**Surprise Package Cupcakes
(p. 81)**

**Sparkling Magic Wands
(p. 94)**

Ice Cream Cone Cupcakes
(p. 82)

Springtime Nests
(p. 96)

Kids' Treats

Banana Split Cupcakes

1 package (18¼ ounces) yellow cake mix, divided
1 cup water
1 cup mashed ripe bananas (about 3 bananas)
3 eggs
1 cup chopped drained maraschino cherries
1½ cups miniature semisweet chocolate chips, divided
1½ cups prepared vanilla frosting
1 cup marshmallow creme
1 teaspoon shortening
30 whole maraschino cherries, drained and patted dry

1. Preheat oven to 350°F. Line 30 standard (2½-inch) muffin cups with paper baking cups.

2. Reserve 2 tablespoons cake mix. Combine remaining cake mix, water, bananas and eggs in large bowl. Beat with electric mixer at low speed about 30 seconds or until moistened. Beat at medium speed 2 minutes. Combine chopped cherries and reserved 2 tablespoons cake mix in small bowl. Stir chopped cherry mixture and 1 cup chocolate chips into batter.

3. Spoon batter into prepared muffin cups, filling two-thirds full. Bake 15 to 20 minutes or until toothpick inserted into centers comes out clean. Cool in pans on wire racks 10 minutes. Remove cupcakes to racks; cool completely.

4. Combine frosting and marshmallow creme in medium bowl until well blended. Frost cupcakes.

5. Combine remaining ½ cup chocolate chips and shortening in small microwavable bowl. Microwave on HIGH 30 to 45 seconds, stirring after 30 seconds, or until smooth. Drizzle over cupcakes. Place 1 whole cherry on each cupcake. *Makes 30 cupcakes*

Variation: Omit chocolate drizzle and top cupcakes with colored sprinkles instead.

Chocolate X and O Cookies

⅔ cup butter or margarine, softened
1 cup sugar
2 teaspoons vanilla extract
2 eggs
2 tablespoons light corn syrup
2½ cups all-purpose flour
½ cup HERSHEY₆S Cocoa
½ teaspoon baking soda
¼ teaspoon salt
Decorating icing

1. Beat butter, sugar and vanilla in large bowl on medium speed of mixer until fluffy. Add eggs; beat well. Beat in corn syrup.

2. Combine flour, cocoa, baking soda and salt; gradually add to butter mixture, beating until well blended. Cover; refrigerate until dough is firm enough to handle.

3. Heat oven to 350°F. Shape dough into X and O shapes.* Place on ungreased cookie sheet.

4. Bake 5 minutes or until set. Remove from cookie sheet to wire rack. Cool completely. Decorate as desired with icing.

Makes about 5 dozen cookies

To shape X's: Shape rounded teaspoons of dough into 3-inch logs. Place 1 log on cookie sheet; press lightly in center. Place another 3-inch log on top of first one, forming X shape. To shape O's: Shape rounded teaspoons dough into 5-inch logs. Connect ends, pressing lightly, forming O shape.

Surprise Package Cupcakes

1 package (18¼ ounces) chocolate (or any flavor) cake mix,
plus ingredients to prepare mix
Food coloring (optional)
1 container (16 ounces) vanilla frosting
1 tube (4¼ ounces) white decorator icing
72 chewy fruit squares
Colored decors and birthday candles (optional)

1. Grease 24 standard (2½-inch) muffin cups or line with paper baking cups. Prepare and bake cake mix in prepared muffin cups according to package directions. Cool in pans on wire racks 15 minutes. Remove cupcakes to racks; cool completely.

2. Tint frosting with food coloring, if desired, adding a few drops at a time until desired color is reached. Spread frosting over cupcakes.

3. Use decorator icing to pipe "ribbons" on fruit squares to resemble wrapped presents. Place 3 candy presents on each cupcake. Decorate with decors and candles, if desired.   *Makes 24 cupcakes*

Take-Along
Snack Mix

1 tablespoon butter or margarine
2 tablespoons honey
1 cup toasted oat cereal, any flavor
½ cup coarsely broken pecans
½ cup thin pretzel sticks, broken in half
½ cup raisins
1 cup "M&M's"® Chocolate Mini Baking Bits

In large heavy skillet over low heat, melt butter. Add honey; stir until blended. Add cereal, nuts, pretzels and raisins; stir until all pieces are evenly coated. Continue cooking over low heat 10 minutes, stirring frequently. Remove from heat; immediately spread on waxed paper until cool. Add "M&M's"® Chocolate Mini Baking Bits. Store in tightly covered container. *Makes about 3½ cups*

Ice Cream Cone Cupcakes

1 package (18¼ ounces) white cake mix, plus ingredients
to prepare mix
2 tablespoons nonpareils
24 flat-bottomed ice cream cones
Prepared vanilla and chocolate frostings
Additional nonpareils and decors

1. Preheat oven to 350°F.

2. Prepare cake mix according to package directions. Stir in 2 tablespoons nonpareils. Spoon ¼ cup batter into each ice cream cone. Stand cones in 13×9-inch baking pan or in muffin pan cups.

3. Bake about 20 minutes or until toothpick inserted into centers comes out clean. Cool completely on wire racks.

4. Frost cupcakes and decorate as desired. *Makes 24 cupcakes*

Note: These cupcakes are best served the day they are prepared. Store them loosely covered.

Shapers

2 packages (20 ounces each) refrigerated sugar cookie dough
Red, yellow, green and blue paste food colorings
1 container (16 ounces) vanilla frosting

1. Remove dough from wrapper. Cut each roll of dough in half.

2. Beat one fourth of dough and red food coloring in medium bowl until well blended. Shape red dough into 5-inch log on sheet of waxed paper; set aside.

3. Repeat with remaining dough and food colorings. Cover; refrigerate tinted logs 1 hour or until firm.

4. Roll or shape each log on smooth surface to create circular-, triangular-, square- and oval-shaped logs. Use ruler to keep triangle and square sides flat. Cover; refrigerate dough 1 hour or until firm.

5. Preheat oven to 350°F. Cut shaped dough into 1/4-inch slices. Place 2 inches apart on ungreased baking sheets. Bake 9 to 12 minutes. Remove to wire racks; cool completely.

6. Spoon frosting into resealable food storage bag; seal. Cut tiny tip from corner of bag. Pipe frosting around each cookie to define shape.

Makes about 6½ dozen cookies

*Tip

Add a little liquid food colorings to the vanilla frosting for an even brighter version of these fun shaped cookies. Use colors that contrast with the cookies—for example green frosting on a red cookie.

Brownie Gems

**1 package DUNCAN HINES® Chocolate Lover's® Double Fudge
   Brownie Mix**
2 eggs
2 tablespoons water
⅓ cup vegetable oil
30 miniature peanut butter cup or chocolate kiss candies
1 container of your favorite Duncan Hines frosting

1. Preheat oven to 350°F. Spray (1¾-inch) mini-muffin pans with vegetable cooking spray or line with foil baking cups.

2. Combine brownie mix, fudge packet from mix, eggs, water and oil in large bowl. Stir with spoon until well blended, about 50 strokes. Drop 1 heaping teaspoonful of batter into each muffin cup; top with candy. Cover candy with more batter. Bake at 350°F for 15 to 17 minutes.

3. Cool 5 minutes. Carefully loosen brownies from pan. Remove to wire racks to cool completely. Frost and decorate as desired.

Makes 30 brownie gems

Candy Corn Cookies

Butter Cookie Dough (recipe follows)
Cookie Glaze (recipe follows)
Yellow and orange food colorings

1. Prepare Butter Cookie Dough.

2. Preheat oven to 350°F. Roll dough on floured surface to ¼-inch thickness. Cut out 3-inch candy corn shapes from dough. Place cutouts on ungreased cookie sheets.

3. Bake 8 to 10 minutes or until edges are lightly browned. Remove to wire racks to cool completely. Prepare Cookie Glaze.

4. Place racks over waxed paper-lined baking sheets. Divide Cookie Glaze into thirds; place in separate small bowls. Tint one third of glaze with yellow food coloring and one third with orange food coloring. Leave remaining glaze white. Spoon glazes over cookies to resemble candy corn. Let stand until glaze is set. *Makes about 2 dozen cookies*

Cookie Glaze: Combine 4 cups powdered sugar and 4 tablespoons milk in small bowl. Add 1 to 2 tablespoons more milk as needed to make medium-thick, pourable glaze.

Butter Cookie Dough

¾ cup (1½ sticks) butter, softened
¼ cup granulated sugar
¼ cup packed light brown sugar
1 egg yolk
1¾ cups all-purpose flour
¾ teaspoon baking powder
⅛ teaspoon salt

1. Beat butter, granulated sugar, brown sugar and egg yolk in medium bowl with electric mixer at medium speed until creamy. Add flour, baking powder and salt; beat until blended.

2. Shape dough into disk; wrap in plastic wrap. Refrigerate about 4 hours or until firm.

Spicy Fruity Popcorn Mix

4 cups lightly salted popped popcorn
2 cups corn cereal squares
1½ cups dried pineapple wedges
1 package (6 ounces) dried fruit bits
Butter-flavored cooking spray
2 tablespoons sugar
1 tablespoon ground cinnamon
1 cup yogurt-covered raisins

1. Preheat oven to 350°F. Combine popcorn, cereal, pineapple and fruit bits in large bowl; mix lightly. Transfer to 15×10-inch jelly-roll pan. Spray mixture generously with cooking spray.

2. Combine sugar and cinnamon in small bowl. Sprinkle half of sugar mixture over popcorn mixture; toss lightly to coat. Spray mixture again with cooking spray. Sprinkle with remaining sugar mixture; mix lightly.

3. Bake 10 minutes, stirring after 5 minutes. Cool completely in pan on wire rack. Add raisins; mix lightly. *Makes about 8½ cups snack mix*

Angel Almond
Cupcakes

1 package DUNCAN HINES® Angel Food Cake Mix
1¼ cups water
2 teaspoons almond extract
1 container DUNCAN HINES® Wild Cherry Vanilla Frosting

1. Preheat oven to 350°F.

2. Combine cake mix, water and almond extract in large bowl. Beat at low speed with electric mixer until moistened. Beat at medium speed for 1 minute. Line medium muffin pans with paper baking cups. Fill muffin cups two-thirds full. Bake at 350°F for 20 to 25 minutes or until golden brown, cracked and dry on top. Remove from muffin pans. Cool completely. Frost and decorate as desired. *Makes 30 to 32 cupcakes*

Cookie Pops

1 package (18 ounces) refrigerated sugar cookie dough
All-purpose flour (optional)
20 (4-inch) lollipop sticks
Assorted frostings, glazes and decors

1. Preheat oven to 350°F. Grease cookie sheets.

2. Remove dough from wrapper. Cut dough in half; refrigerate one half. Sprinkle remaining dough with flour to minimize sticking, if necessary. Roll to ⅛-inch thickness on lightly floured surface. Cut dough using 3½-inch cookie cutters.

3. Place lollipop sticks on cutouts so that tips of sticks are embedded in dough. Carefully turn cutouts so sticks are in back; place on prepared cookie sheets. Repeat with remaining dough and sticks.

4. Bake 7 to 11 minutes or until edges are lightly browned. Cool cookies on cookie sheets 2 minutes. Remove cookies to wire racks; cool completely.

5. Decorate as desired. *Makes 20 cookies*

Indian Corn

¼ cup (½ stick) butter or margarine
1 package (10½ ounces) mini marshmallows
Yellow food coloring
8 cups peanut butter and chocolate puffed corn cereal
1 cup candy-coated chocolate pieces, divided
10 lollipop sticks
Tan and green raffia

1. Line large baking sheet with waxed paper; set aside.

2. Melt butter in large heavy saucepan over low heat. Add marshmallows; stir until melted and smooth. Tint with food coloring until desired shade is reached. Add cereal and ½ cup chocolate pieces; stir until evenly coated. Remove from heat.

3. With lightly greased hands, quickly divide mixture into 10 oblong pieces. Push lollipop stick halfway into each piece; shape like ear of corn. Place on prepared baking sheet. Press remaining ½ cup chocolate pieces into each ear. Let treats stand until set.

4. Tie or tape raffia to lollipop sticks to resemble corn husks.

Makes 10 servings

*Tip
Lollipop sticks and colored raffia are sold at craft and hobby stores.

Space Dust Bars

1 package (12 ounces) white chocolate chips
⅓ cup butter
2 cups graham cracker crumbs
1 cup chopped pecans
2 cans (12 ounces each) apricot pastry filling
1 cup flaked coconut
  Additional flaked coconut or powdered sugar (optional)

1. Preheat oven to 350°F. Grease 13×9-inch baking pan.

2. Combine white chocolate chips and butter in medium heavy saucepan; cook and stir over very low heat until melted and smooth. Remove from heat; stir in graham cracker crumbs and pecans. Let cool 5 minutes.

3. Press half of crumb mixture onto bottom of prepared pan. Bake 10 minutes or until golden brown.

4. Remove from oven; spread apricot filling evenly over crust. Combine coconut and remaining crumb mixture; sprinkle evenly over filling.

5. Bake 20 to 25 minutes or until light golden brown. Cool completely in pan on wire rack. Sprinkle with additional coconut or powdered sugar, if desired. Cut into bars. *Makes 1½ dozen bars*

*Tip

Bring these bars to a space-themed birthday party or give them with a space-themed gift. To use as place cards or party favors, cut the bars into circles and put one at each place setting. Stand a small plastic astronaut, holding a paper flag with the guest's name, on the center of each circle.

Domino Cookies

1 package (18 ounces) refrigerated sugar cookie dough
All-purpose flour (optional)
½ cup semisweet chocolate chips

1. Preheat oven to 350°F. Grease cookie sheets.

2. Remove dough from wrapper. Cut dough into 4 equal pieces. Reserve 1 piece; refrigerate remaining 3 pieces.

3. Roll reserved dough to ⅛-inch thickness. Sprinkle with flour to minimize sticking, if necessary. Cut out 9 (2½×1¾-inch) rectangles using sharp knife. Place 2 inches apart on prepared cookie sheets.

4. Score each cookie across middle with sharp knife. Gently press chocolate chips, point side down, into dough to resemble various dominos. Repeat with remaining dough, scraps and chocolate chips.

5. Bake 8 to 10 minutes or until edges are light golden brown. Remove to wire racks; cool completely. *Makes 3 dozen cookies*

Sparkling Magic Wands

1 package (18 ounces) refrigerated sugar cookie dough
48 pretzel sticks (2½ inches long)
Prepared colored decorating icings
Colored sugar or edible glitter and gold dragées

1. Preheat oven to 350°F.

2. Roll dough to ⅛-inch thickness on well-floured surface. Cut dough with 2-inch star-shaped cookie cutter. Place each star on top of 1 pretzel stick; press lightly to attach. Place on ungreased cookie sheet.

3. Bake 4 to 6 minutes or until edges are lightly browned. Carefully remove to wire racks; cool completely.

4. Spread icing on stars; sprinkle with colored sugar. Press dragées into points of stars. Let stand until set. *Makes 4 dozen cookies*

Meringue Bone Cookies

1½ cups sugar
  Pinch of salt
  5 egg whites, at room temperature
  Pinch of cream of tartar
  1 teaspoon almond, vanilla, orange or lemon extract

1. Preheat oven to 220°F. Line 2 cookie sheets with parchment paper. Prepare pastry bag with round #10 tip (about ⅜-inch diameter).

2. Combine sugar and salt in small bowl. Beat egg whites and cream of tartar in medium bowl with electric mixer at medium speed until soft peaks form. Gradually add sugar mixture, beating constantly. Beat until stiff peaks form and meringue is glossy and smooth. Add extract; beat just until blended.

3. Fill pastry bag with meringue. Pipe log 3 to 4 inches long. Pipe 2 balls on both ends of each log. Smooth any peaks with wet finger. Repeat with remaining meringue. Bake 30 minutes; turn off heat. Leave cookies in oven overnight; do not open oven door.   *Makes about 2 dozen cookies*

Tip: To give the bones an ivory or aged look, add 1 to 2 drops yellow food coloring with the extract.

Caramel Corn Apple-O's

7 cups popped butter-flavor microwave popcorn
2¼ cups apple-cinnamon ring cereal
½ cup chopped dried apples or apricots
¼ cup chopped nuts (optional)
1 package (14 ounces) caramels
2 tablespoons butter or margarine
1 to 2 tablespoons water
Long cinnamon sticks or wooden craft sticks (optional)

1. Combine popcorn, cereal, dried apples and nuts, if desired, in large bowl. Place caramels, butter and water in large microwavable bowl; microwave on HIGH 2½ to 3 minutes or until melted and smooth, stirring after each minute.

2. Pour caramel mixture over popcorn mixture; toss with buttered wooden spoon to coat. Let set until cool enough to handle.

3. With damp hands, shape mixture into 8 balls around cinnamon sticks. Place on buttered waxed paper until ready to serve.   *Makes 8 balls*

Springtime Nests

1 cup butterscotch chips
½ cup *each* light corn syrup and creamy peanut butter
⅓ cup sugar
2½ cups chow mein noodles
2 cups cornflakes, lightly crushed
Jelly beans or malted milk egg candies

1. Combine butterscotch chips, corn syrup, peanut butter and sugar in large microwavable bowl. Microwave on HIGH 1 to 1½ minutes or until melted and smooth, stirring at 30-second intervals.

2. Stir in chow mein noodles and cornflakes until evenly coated. Quickly shape scant ¼ cupfuls of mixture into balls; make indentation in centers to create nests. Place nests on waxed paper to set. Place 3 jelly beans in each nest.   *Makes 1½ dozen treats*

Frosted Buttermilk Brownie
Squares (p. 112)

Taffy Apple Cookies
(p. 123)

Nutty Orzo and Rice Pilaf
(p. 118)

Happy Birthday Cookies
(p. 102)

Jar Gifts

Sweet Potato Muffins Mix

2 cups flour
1 tablespoon baking powder
1 teaspoon ground cinnamon
½ teaspoon baking soda
½ teaspoon salt
¼ teaspoon ground nutmeg
½ cup packed brown sugar
¾ cup chopped walnuts
¾ cup golden raisins

1. Combine flour, baking powder, cinnamon, baking soda, salt and nutmeg in large bowl. Layer flour mixture, brown sugar, walnuts and raisins in 1-quart food storage jar with tight-fitting lid. Pack ingredients down lightly before adding another layer.

2. Seal jar. Cover top of jar with fabric; attach gift tag with preparation instructions to jar with raffia or ribbon. *Makes 1 (1-quart) jar*

Sweet Potato Muffins

1 cup mashed cooked sweet potato
¾ cup milk
½ cup (1 stick) butter, melted
2 eggs, beaten
1½ teaspoons vanilla
Sweet Potato Muffins Mix

1. Preheat oven to 400°F. Grease 24 standard (2½-inch) muffin cups. Combine sweet potato, milk, butter, eggs and vanilla in large bowl. Stir in muffin mix just until combined.

2. Spoon batter evenly into prepared muffin cups. Bake 15 minutes or until toothpick inserted into centers comes out clean. Cool in pans 5 minutes; remove to wire racks. *Makes 24 muffins*

Happy Birthday Cookie Mix

1¼ cups flour
½ teaspoon baking powder
¼ teaspoon baking soda
¼ teaspoon salt
⅓ cup packed brown sugar
⅓ cup granulated sugar
¾ cup mini candy-coated chocolate pieces
½ cup chocolate-covered toffee chips
½ cup peanut butter and milk chocolate chips
½ cup lightly salted peanuts, coarsely chopped

1. Combine flour, baking powder, baking soda and salt in large bowl. Spoon flour mixture into 1-quart food storage jar with tight-fitting lid. Layer remaining ingredients on top of flour. Pack ingredients down lightly before adding another layer.

2. Seal jar. Cover top of jar with fabric; attach gift tag with preparation instructions to jar with raffia or ribbon. *Makes 1 (1-quart) jar*

Happy Birthday Cookies

½ cup (1 stick) butter, softened
1 egg
½ teaspoon vanilla
Happy Birthday Cookie Mix

1. Preheat oven to 375°F. Line cookie sheets with parchment paper.

2. Beat butter in large bowl with electric mixer at medium speed until fluffy. Beat in egg and vanilla. Add cookie mix to butter mixture; beat 1 minute or until light dough forms.

3. Drop dough by rounded tablespoonfuls 2 inches apart onto prepared cookie sheets. Bake 10 minutes or until firm and golden brown. Let cookies stand 1 minute. Remove to wire racks; cool completely.
Makes 3 dozen cookies

Asian Spicy Sweet Mustard

1 jar (16 ounces) spicy brown mustard
1 cup peanut butter
¾ cup hoisin sauce
½ cup packed brown sugar

1. Combine mustard, peanut butter, hoisin sauce and brown sugar in medium bowl. Blend with wire whisk.

2. Spoon into 4 labeled 1-cup containers. Store refrigerated up to 4 weeks.   *Makes 4 (1-cup) containers*

Cracked Peppercorn Honey Mustard

2½ cups Dijon mustard
1 jar (9½ ounces) extra-grainy Dijon mustard
¾ cup honey
2 tablespoons cracked black pepper
1 tablespoon dried tarragon leaves (optional)

1. Combine Dijon mustard, extra-grainy Dijon mustard, honey, pepper and tarragon, if desired, in medium bowl. Blend with wire whisk.

2. Spoon into 4 labeled 1¼-cup containers. Store refrigerated up to 4 weeks.   *Makes 4 (1¼-cup) containers*

Layered Bean Soup Mix

½ **cup dried black-eyed peas**
½ **cup dried black beans**
½ **cup dried lentils**
½ **cup dried pinto beans**
½ **cup dried green split peas**
½ **cup dried white beans**
½ **cup dried pink or red beans**
¼ **cup dried chopped or minced onion**
¼ **cup dried parsley flakes**
1 **teaspoon** *each* **garlic powder and dried basil**
6 **vegetable bouillon cubes, unwrapped**
2 **whole bay leaves**

1. Layer beans, lentils and peas in 1-quart food storage jar with tight-fitting lid. Combine seasonings in small bowl and place in resealable food storage bag with bouillon and bay leaves; place bag in jar.

2. Seal jar. Cover top of jar with fabric; attach gift tag with preparation instructions to jar with raffia or ribbon.   *Makes 1 (1-quart) jar*

Layered Bean Soup

Layered Bean Soup Mix
8 **cups water**
**Chopped tomatoes, chopped cilantro, shredded
    mozzarella cheese or sour cream (optional)**

1. Remove seasoning packet from jar. Place beans in 5- to 6-quart stock pot; add enough water to cover by 1 inch. Bring to a boil over high heat; reduce heat and simmer, covered, 5 minutes. Turn off heat and let beans sit, covered, for 1 hour; drain.

2. Add 8 cups water and contents of seasoning packet. Bring to a boil over high heat. Cover; reduce heat. Simmer 1½ hours or until beans are tender.

3. Remove 1 cup soup to a bowl; mash with a fork. Return mashed beans to pot. Simmer, uncovered, 30 minutes, stirring occasionally. Remove bay leaves. Garnish each serving as desired.   *Makes 8 servings*

Cranberry-Pecan Muffins Mix

1¾ cups all-purpose flour
1 cup dried cranberries
¾ cup chopped pecans
½ cup packed light brown sugar
2½ teaspoons baking powder
½ teaspoon salt

1. Place flour in 1-quart food storage jar with tight-fitting lid. Layer remaining ingredients on top of flour. Pack ingredients down lightly before adding another layer.

2. Seal jar. Cover top of jar with fabric; attach gift tag with preparation instructions to jar with raffia or ribbon. *Makes 1 (1-quart) jar*

Cranberry-Pecan Muffins

Cranberry-Pecan Muffins Mix
¾ cup milk
¼ cup (½ stick) butter, melted
1 egg, beaten

1. Preheat oven to 400°F. Grease 12 standard (2½-inch) muffin cups or line with paper baking cups.

2. Pour muffin mix into large bowl. Combine milk, melted butter and egg in small bowl until blended; stir into muffin mix just until moistened. Spoon evenly into prepared muffin cups.

3. Bake 16 to 18 minutes or until toothpick inserted into centers comes out clean. Cool in pan on wire rack 5 minutes. Remove from pan; cool completely on wire rack. *Makes 12 muffins*

Easy Cocoa Mix

2 cups nonfat dry milk powder
1 cup sugar
¾ cup powdered nondairy creamer
½ cup unsweetened cocoa powder
¼ teaspoon salt

1. Combine all ingredients in medium bowl until well blended. Spoon into 1-quart food storage jar with tight-fitting lid.

2. Seal jar. Cover top of jar with fabric; attach gift tag with serving instructions to jar with raffia or ribbon.

Makes about 4 cups mix (16 servings)

For single serving: Place rounded ¼ cup Easy Cocoa Mix in mug; add ¾ cup boiling water. Stir until mix is dissolved. Top with sweetened whipped cream and marshmallows, if desired. Serve immediately.

Super Chocolate Cookies Mix

1½ cups all-purpose flour
1 cup packed light brown sugar
¾ cup candy-coated chocolate pieces
½ cup salted peanuts
½ cup raisins
¼ cup unsweetened cocoa powder
¾ teaspoon baking soda
¼ teaspoon salt

1. Place flour in 1-quart food storage jar with tight-fitting lid. Layer remaining ingredients on top of flour. Pack ingredients down lightly before adding another layer.

2. Seal jar. Cover top of jar with fabric; attach gift tag with preparation instructions to jar with raffia or ribbon. *Makes 1 (1-quart) jar*

Super Chocolate Cookies

⅔ cup butter, softened
2 eggs
1½ teaspoons vanilla
Super Chocolate Cookies Mix

1. Preheat oven to 350°F.

2. Beat butter in large bowl with electric mixer at medium speed until smooth. Beat in eggs and vanilla until blended. (Mixture may appear curdled.) Add cookie mix to butter mixture; stir until well blended.

3. Drop heaping tablespoonfuls of dough 2 inches apart onto ungreased cookie sheets. Bake 11 to 12 minutes or until almost set. Let cookies stand on cookie sheets 2 minutes. Remove cookies to wire racks; cool completely. *Makes 2 dozen cookies*

Super Chocolate Cookies

⅓ cup butter, soften
2 eggs
1½ teaspoons vanilla
1 jar Super Chocolate Cookie

Preheat oven to 350°F.

Beat butter in large bowl until smooth. Beat in egg, water and vanilla until well blended. Add contents of jar to butter mixture; stir until well blended.

Drop rounded teaspoonfuls of dough 2 inches apart onto prepared cookie sheets. Bake 8 to 10 minutes or until edges are golden brown. Remove cookie sheets. Bake 8 to 10 minutes.

Hearty Lentil & Barley Soup Mix

¾ cup dried brown or red lentils
¼ cup sun-dried tomato halves (not packed in oil), chopped
2 tablespoons dried vegetable flakes, soup greens or
    dehydrated vegetables*
1 tablespoon dried minced onion
2 teaspoons chicken bouillon granules
1 teaspoon dried oregano
½ teaspoon dried minced garlic
½ teaspoon black pepper
⅛ teaspoon red pepper flakes (optional)
½ cup uncooked medium pearled barley

*Vegetable flakes and soup greens are available in the spice section of large supermarkets. Or, look for dried vegetable flakes (bell peppers, carrots, etc.) in the bulk food section of specialty food markets.

1. Layer lentils, tomatoes, vegetable flakes, onion, bouillon, oregano, garlic, black pepper, red pepper flakes and barley in 1-pint food storage jar with tight-fitting lid.

2. Seal jar. Cover top of jar with fabric; attach gift tag with preparation instructions to jar with raffia or ribbon. *Makes 1 (1-pint) jar*

Hearty Lentil & Barley Soup

    Hearty Lentil & Barley Soup Mix
5 to 6 cups water
1 can (about 14 ounces) diced tomatoes with green pepper,
    celery and onion
½ pound smoked sausage, cut into ½-inch slices

Slow Cooker Directions
Place soup mix, water, tomatoes and sausage in slow cooker; stir. Cover and cook on LOW 6 to 8 hours. Add additional water, ½ cup at a time, if needed to reach desired consistency. *Makes 10 to 12 servings*

Conventional Method: Simmer all ingredients in Dutch oven, partially covered, 1 to 1½ hours or until lentils are tender.

Frosted Buttermilk Brownie Squares Mix

Brownies
- 2 cups all-purpose flour
- ¼ cup unsweetened cocoa powder
- 1 teaspoon baking soda
- 2 cups granulated sugar
- 1 cup chopped walnuts

Frosting
- 4½ cups powdered sugar
- ¼ cup unsweetened cocoa powder

1. For brownie mix jar, whisk together flour, cocoa and baking soda in medium bowl. Place mixture in 1-quart food storage jar with tight-fitting lid, packing down lightly as needed. Layer granulated sugar and walnuts on top of flour mixture.

2. For frosting jar, combine powdered sugar and cocoa in large bowl. Place mixture in 1-quart food storage jar with tight-fitting lid, ¾ cup at a time. Pack down lightly before adding another layer.

3. Seal jars. Cover tops of jars with fabric; attach gift tag with preparation instructions to jars with raffia or ribbon.   *Makes 2 (1-quart) jars*

Frosted Buttermilk Brownie Squares

Brownies
- Frosted Buttermilk Brownie Squares Mix
- 1 cup boiling water
- ½ cup (1 stick) unsalted butter, melted
- ½ cup vegetable oil
- ½ cup buttermilk
- 2 eggs
- 1 teaspoon vanilla

Frosting
- Buttermilk Frosting Mix
- ½ cup (1 stick) unsalted butter, melted
- ½ cup buttermilk
- 1 teaspoon vanilla

1. Preheat oven to 375°F. Line bottom and sides of jelly-roll pan with parchment paper, extending slightly over edges of pan. Spray paper with nonstick cooking spray.

2. For brownies, place brownie mix in large bowl; whisk to combine dry ingredients. Add water, butter, oil, buttermilk, eggs and vanilla; stir to combine. Spread batter in prepared pan. Bake 20 to 23 minutes or until toothpick inserted into center comes out clean. Cool completely in pan on wire rack.

3. For frosting, place frosting mix in medium bowl; whisk to break up any lumps. Add butter, buttermilk and vanilla; whisk until smooth. Let frosting stand about 15 minutes. Spread over brownies. Refrigerate until set. Cut into squares. *Makes about 36 brownies*

Mocha Coffee Mix

1 cup nonfat dry milk powder
¾ cup granulated sugar
⅔ cup powdered nondairy creamer
½ cup unsweetened cocoa powder
⅓ cup instant coffee, pressed through fine sieve
¼ cup packed light brown sugar
1 teaspoon ground cinnamon
¼ teaspoon salt
¼ teaspoon ground nutmeg

1. Combine all ingredients in medium bowl until well blended. Place in 1-quart food storage jar with tight-fitting lid.

2. Seal jar. Cover top of jar with fabric; attach gift tag with serving instructions to jar with raffia or ribbon.
Makes about 3½ cups mix (10 to 12 servings)

For single serving: Place rounded ¼ cup Mocha Coffee Mix in mug; add ¾ cup boiling water. Stir until mix is dissolved. Serve immediately.

Pumpkin Chocolate Chip Muffin Mix

2½ cups all-purpose flour
1 cup packed light brown sugar
1 cup (6 ounces) chocolate chips
½ cup chopped walnuts
1 tablespoon baking powder
1½ teaspoons pumpkin pie spice*
¼ teaspoon salt

Substitute ¾ teaspoon ground cinnamon, ⅜ teaspoon ground ginger and scant ¼ teaspoon each ground allspice and ground nutmeg for 1½ teaspoons pumpkin pie spice.

1. Place flour in 1-quart food storage jar with tight-fitting lid. Layer remaining ingredients on top of flour. Pack ingredients down lightly before adding another layer.

2. Seal jar. Cover top of jar with fabric; attach gift tag with preparation instructions to jar with raffia or ribbon. *Makes 1 (1-quart) jar*

Pumpkin Chocolate Chip Muffins

Pumpkin Chocolate Chip Muffin Mix
1 cup solid-pack pumpkin
¾ cup milk
6 tablespoons butter, melted
2 eggs

1. Preheat oven to 400°F. Grease 18 standard (2½-inch) muffin cups or line with paper baking cups.

2. Pour muffin mix into large bowl. Combine pumpkin, milk, butter and eggs in small bowl until blended; stir into jar mixture just until moistened. Spoon evenly into prepared muffin cups, filling two-thirds full.

3. Bake 15 to 17 minutes or until toothpick inserted into centers comes out clean. Cool in pans on wire racks 10 minutes. Remove from pans; cool on wire racks. *Makes 18 muffins*

Crunchy Curried Snack Mix

2½ cups rice cereal squares
¾ cup walnut halves
¾ cup dried cranberries or dried cherries
2 tablespoons packed brown sugar
1½ teaspoons curry powder
¼ teaspoon ground cumin
¼ teaspoon salt

1. Layer 1¼ cups cereal, walnuts, cranberries and remaining 1¼ cups cereal in 2-quart food storage jar with tight-fitting lid. Combine brown sugar, curry powder, cumin and salt in small food storage bag. Close with twist tie and cut off top of bag. Place bag on top of cereal.

2. Seal jar. Cover top of jar with fabric; attach gift tag with preparation instructions to jar with raffia or ribbon. *Makes 1 (2-quart) jar*

Gift Idea: Assemble a gift basket with a jar of Crunchy Curried Snack Mix and a favorite bottle of wine or a selection of specialty beers or sodas.

Crunchy Curried Snack Mix

Crunchy Curried Snack Mix
6 tablespoons butter

1. Preheat oven to 250°F. Remove seasoning packet from jar.

2. Melt butter in large skillet. Add contents of seasoning packet; mix well. Add remaining contents of jar; stir to coat. Spread mixture evenly on ungreased jelly-roll pan. Bake 40 to 45 minutes or until crispy, stirring every 15 minutes. *Makes 6 cups snack mix*

Note: To crisp in slow cooker, spoon snack mix into slow cooker. Cover and cook on LOW 3 hours. Remove cover; cook additional 30 minutes.

Nutty Orzo and Rice Pilaf Mix

¾ cup uncooked orzo pasta
3 tablespoons dried vegetable flakes, soup greens or dehydrated vegetables*
2 teaspoons chicken bouillon granules
½ teaspoon dried thyme
¼ teaspoon black pepper
½ cup uncooked instant brown rice
½ cup pecan pieces

Vegetable flakes and soup greens are available in the spice section of large supermarkets. Or, look for dried vegetable flakes (bell peppers, carrots, etc.) in the bulk food section of specialty food markets.

1. Layer orzo, vegetable flakes, bouillon granules, thyme, pepper and rice in 1-pint food storage jar with tight-fitting lid. Place pecans in small food storage bag. Close with twist tie and cut off top of bag. Place bag on top of rice.

2. Seal jar. Cover top of jar with fabric; attach gift tag with preparation instructions to jar with raffia or ribbon. *Makes 1 (1-pint) jar*

Nutty Orzo and Rice Pilaf

Nutty Orzo and Rice Pilaf Mix
2 cups water
1 tablespoon butter

1. Preheat oven to 350°F. Remove pecan packet from jar; set aside.

2. Combine water, butter and soup mix in large saucepan. Bring to a boil over high heat. Cover; reduce heat and simmer 10 to 15 minutes or until orzo is tender.

3. Meanwhile, spread pecans in single layer on ungreased baking sheet. Bake 5 to 8 minutes or until nuts just begin to darken.

4. Stir pecans into pilaf. Cook, uncovered, 2 to 3 minutes or until heated through. *Makes 4 to 5 servings*

Variation: Add 1 cup cooked carrots, peas or asparagus in step 4.

Double Chocolate Walnut Bread Mix

2¾ cups all-purpose flour
3 tablespoons unsweetened cocoa powder
2½ teaspoons baking powder
2 teaspoons baking soda
1 teaspoon salt
1 cup sugar
½ cup chocolate chips
½ cup walnuts, coarsely chopped

1. Combine flour, cocoa, baking powder, baking soda and salt in medium bowl. Place flour mixture in 1-quart food storage jar with tight-fitting lid. Layer remaining ingredients over flour mixture. Pack ingredients down lightly before adding another layer.

2. Seal jar. Cover top of jar with fabric; attach gift tag with preparation instructions to jar with raffia or ribbon. *Makes 1 (1-quart) jar*

Double Chocolate Walnut Bread

Double Chocolate Walnut Bread Mix
1½ cups milk
⅓ cup vegetable oil
1 egg, beaten
1½ teaspoons vanilla

1. Preheat oven to 350°F. Spray 2 (8½×4½-inch) loaf pans with nonstick cooking spray.

2. Pour muffin mix into large bowl. Combine milk, oil, egg and vanilla in small bowl until blended; stir into muffin mix just until moistened. Pour evenly into prepared pans; smooth tops.

3. Bake 45 to 50 minutes or until toothpick inserted into centers comes out clean. Cool in pans on wire racks 15 minutes. Remove from pans; cool on wire racks. *Makes 2 loaves*

Mixed Berry Muffin Mix

2¼ cups cake flour
¾ teaspoon baking soda
½ teaspoon salt
½ teaspoon ground nutmeg
¼ teaspoon ground cardamom
¼ teaspoon ground ginger
¾ cup granulated sugar
2 cups dried mixed berries (cranberries, cherries, blueberries, strawberries)

1. Whisk together flour, baking soda, salt, nutmeg, cardamom and ginger in medium bowl. Place mixture in 1-quart food storage jar with tight-fitting lid, packing down occasionally. Place sugar and berries in separate resealable food storage bags; add bags to jar.

2. Seal jar. Cover top of jar with fabric; attach gift tag with preparation instructions to jar with raffia or ribbon. *Makes 1 (1-quart) jar*

Mixed Berry Muffins

Mixed Berry Muffin Mix
½ cup (1 stick) unsalted butter, softened
1 cup buttermilk
2 eggs

1. Preheat oven to 375°F. Grease 12 standard (2½-inch) muffin cups or line with paper baking cups.

2. Remove sugar and berry packets from jar. Place contents of sugar packet in medium bowl. Add butter, buttermilk and eggs. Beat with electric mixer at medium speed until creamy. Add remaining mix, one third at a time, mixing well after each addition. Stir in dried berries.

3. Spoon batter into prepared muffin cups, filling one-third full. Bake 15 to 20 minutes or until toothpick inserted into centers of muffins comes out clean. Cool in pan on wire rack 5 minutes. Remove from pan; cool on wire rack. *Makes 12 muffins*

Taffy Apple Cookie Mix

1½ cups all-purpose flour
1 teaspoon baking soda
¼ teaspoon baking powder
¼ teaspoon salt
¾ cup packed light brown sugar
1½ cups butterscotch chips
1 cup dried apples

1. Combine flour, baking soda, baking powder and salt in large bowl. Layer flour mixture, brown sugar, butterscotch chips and dried apples in 1-quart food storage jar with tight-fitting lid. Pack ingredients down slightly before adding each layer.

2. Seal jar. Cover top of jar with fabric; attach gift tag with preparation instructions to jar with raffia or ribbon. *Makes 1 (1-quart) jar*

Taffy Apple Cookies

½ cup (1 stick) butter, softened
½ cup chunky peanut butter
1 egg
Taffy Apple Cookie Mix
1 cup caramel apple dip
½ cup chopped peanuts

1. Preheat oven to 350°F. Beat butter and peanut butter in large bowl with electric mixer at medium speed until smooth. Add egg and cookie mix; beat until well blended.

2. Drop dough by rounded tablespoonfuls 2 inches apart onto ungreased cookie sheets. Bake 8 to 10 minutes or until edges are lightly browned. Cool cookies 2 minutes on cookie sheets. Remove to wire rack; cool completely.

3. Spread about 1 teaspoon caramel apple dip onto each cookie. Sprinkle with chopped peanuts. *Makes about 4 dozen cookies*

Crispy Holiday Treats Mix

1 cup powdered sugar
1½ cups crisp rice cereal
½ cup chopped dried tart cherries
¾ cup mini semisweet chocolate chips
¼ cup chopped toasted pecans
¾ cup flaked coconut

1. Layer all ingredients except coconut in the order listed above in 1-quart food storage jar with tight-fitting lid. Pack ingredients down firmly before adding another layer. Place coconut in small food storage bag. Close with twist tie; cut off top of bag. Place bag in jar.

2. Seal jar. Cover top of jar with fabric; attach gift tag with preparation instructions to jar with raffia or ribbon.   *Makes 1 (1-quart) jar*

Gift Idea: Fill a holiday gift bag with a jar of Crispy Holiday Treats Mix, a package of small candy cups and a decorative candy dish.

Crispy Holiday Treats

Crispy Holiday Treats Mix
1 cup peanut butter
¼ cup (½ stick) butter, softened

1. Remove coconut packet from jar. Place remaining contents of jar in large bowl; stir. Combine peanut butter and butter in medium bowl until well blended; add to cereal mixture. Stir until well blended.

2. Shape rounded teaspoonfuls of dough into 1½-inch balls. Roll balls in coconut. Store in single layer in refrigerator.   *Makes about 24 treats*

Crispy Holiday Treats

1 jar Crispy Holiday Treats Mix
1 cup creamy butter
¼ cup butter softened

1. Remove coconut from jar. Place remaining contents of jar into large
mix well. Beat together peanut butter and butter in medium bowl un
combined. Add to cereal mixture; mix well.

2. Shape teaspoonfuls of mixture into 1-inch balls. R3
in food storage container. Refrigerate 1 ho

Date Nut Bread
(p. 144)

Rice Pudding
(p. 141)

**Mushroom Soup with
Croutons (p. 130)**

**Pineapple Upside-Down
Mini Cake (p. 148)**

Mug Recipes

Chocolate Fudge Cake Mix

3 tablespoons all-purpose flour
3 tablespoons semisweet chocolate chips
2 tablespoons granulated sugar
2 tablespoons packed brown sugar
2 tablespoons unsweetened cocoa powder
⅛ teaspoon baking powder
Pinch salt

1. Combine all ingredients in small bowl. Spoon into small food storage bag. Seal; place in 1½-cup microwave-safe mug.

2. Decorate mug and attach gift tag with preparation instructions.

Makes 1 mix

Chocolate Fudge Cake

¼ cup milk
3 tablespoons butter, melted and cooled
¼ teaspoon vanilla
Chocolate Fudge Cake Mix
Vanilla ice cream (optional)
Colored sprinkles (optional)

1. Combine milk, butter and vanilla in medium bowl; stir until well blended. Add cake mix; stir until smooth.

2. Spray inside of mug with nonstick cooking spray; spoon batter into mug. Microwave on HIGH 2 minutes. Let cake stand 3 to 4 minutes. Serve immediately, topped with vanilla ice cream and colored sprinkles, if desired.

Makes 1 to 2 servings

Mushroom Soup with Croutons Mix

2 tablespoons thin egg noodles
2 tablespoons chopped dried shiitake mushrooms
1½ teaspoons beef bouillon granules
1 teaspoon dried parsley flakes
1 teaspoon dried chopped carrot
½ teaspoon dried celery flakes
½ teaspoon dried minced onion
3 tablespoons small seasoned croutons

1. Combine noodles, mushrooms, bouillon granules, parsley, carrot, celery and onion in small bowl. Spoon into small food storage bag. Seal; place in 1½-cup mug. Place croutons in separate small food storage bag. Seal; place in mug.

2. Decorate mug and attach gift tag with preparation instructions.

Makes 1 mix

Mushroom Soup with Croutons

Mushroom Soup with Croutons Mix
2 cups water

1. Remove bag of croutons from mug; set aside. Combine water and soup mix in small saucepan. Bring to a boil over high heat; stir.

2. Reduce heat to medium; simmer 30 minutes or until mushrooms are tender. Sprinkle with reserved croutons just before serving.

Makes 1 serving

Mocha Pudding
Mix

⅓ cup sugar
2 tablespoons cornstarch
2 tablespoons unsweetened cocoa powder
1 teaspoon espresso powder or instant coffee granules
⅛ teaspoon salt

1. Combine sugar, cornstarch, cocoa powder, espresso powder and salt in small bowl; stir until blended. Spoon into small food storage bag. Seal; place in 1½-cup mug.

2. Decorate mug and attach gift tag with preparation instructions.
Makes 1 mix

Mocha Pudding

Mocha Pudding Mix
1¼ cups milk
1 tablespoon butter
½ teaspoon vanilla

1. Place pudding mix in small saucepan; whisk in milk. Cook over medium heat, whisking constantly, until large bubbles form.

2. Reduce heat to low; whisk in butter and vanilla until well blended. Pour into mug to cool. Serve warm or press plastic wrap onto pudding surface and refrigerate about 1 hour or until cold. *Makes 1 serving*

Mocha Pudding Mix
Place pudding mix in a small saucepan and
whisk in milk. Place saucepan over medium heat
whisk constantly until begin
reduce hea

Clam Chowder Mix

1 can (6½ ounces) clams
⅓ cup instant mashed potato flakes
½ teaspoon dried onion flakes
¼ teaspoon dried parsley flakes
⅛ teaspoon white pepper
3 tablespoons oyster crackers

1. Place unopened can of clams in 1½-cup microwave-safe mug. Combine potato flakes, onion flakes, parsley flakes and pepper in small bowl. Spoon into small food storage bag; seal. Place in mug. Place oyster crackers in separate small food storage bag; seal. Place in mug.

2. Decorate mug and attach gift tag with preparation instructions.

Makes 1 mix

Clam Chowder

Clam Chowder Mix
¾ cup milk
1 tablespoon butter
⅛ teaspoon paprika (optional)

1. Remove bag of crackers from mug; set aside. Pour can of clams, including liquid, into mug. Stir in soup mix, milk and butter. Cover mug with vented plastic wrap. Microwave on HIGH 1 minute; stir.

2. Microwave 1 minute more or until creamy and heated through; stir. Sprinkle with paprika, if desired. Serve with reserved oyster crackers.

Makes 1 serving

Tortellini Soup Mix

½ cup uncooked dried tortellini
1 tablespoon finely chopped dried mushrooms
2 teaspoons minced sun-dried tomatoes (not packed in oil)
1½ teaspoons chicken bouillon granules
¼ teaspoon Italian seasoning
⅛ teaspoon dried parsley flakes

1. Combine tortellini, mushrooms, tomatoes, bouillon granules, seasoning and parsley in small bowl. Spoon into small food storage bag. Seal; place bag in 1½-cup mug.

2. Decorate mug and attach gift tag with preparation instructions.

Makes 1 mix

Tortellini Soup

1½ cups water
Tortellini Soup Mix

1. Combine water and soup mix in small saucepan. Bring to a boil over high heat; stir.

2. Reduce heat to medium; simmer gently 11 minutes or until tortellini are tender.

Makes 1 serving

Fruit Crumble Mix

2 tablespoons granulated sugar
1 teaspoon cornstarch
¾ teaspoon ground cinnamon, divided
¾ cup all-purpose flour
¾ cup packed brown sugar
¼ teaspoon salt

1. Combine granulated sugar, cornstarch and ¼ teaspoon cinnamon in small bowl. Spoon into small food storage bag. Seal; label "filling" and place in 1½-cup mug.

2. Combine flour, brown sugar, remaining ½ teaspoon cinnamon and salt in small bowl. Spoon into separate small food storage bag. Seal; label "topping" and place in mug. Decorate mug and attach gift tag with preparation instructions.   *Makes 1 mix*

Fruit Crumble

1 pound assorted fresh or frozen fruit (such peaches, blueberries, raspberries or blackberries)
2 tablespoons water
Fruit Crumble Mix
5 tablespoons butter, divided

1. Preheat oven to 350°F. Spray 9-inch pie plate with nonstick cooking spray. Place fruit and water in prepared plate and sprinkle with filling; stir gently. Dot top of fruit mixture with 1 tablespoon butter.

2. Place topping in small bowl; cut in remaining 4 tablespoons butter, using pastry blender or 2 knives, until mixture is crumbly. Mound topping over fruit mixture. Bake 40 minutes or until bubbly.   *Makes 4 servings*

Apricot
Mini Muffin Mix

¾ cup all-purpose flour
¼ cup sugar
¼ cup finely chopped dried apricots
⅛ teaspoon baking powder
⅛ teaspoon baking soda
   Pinch ground nutmeg
   Pinch salt

1. Combine all ingredients in small bowl. Spoon into small food storage bag. Seal; place in 1½-cup mug.

2. Decorate mug and attach gift tag with preparation instructions.

Makes 1 mix

Apricot Mini Muffins

¼ cup (½ stick) butter, melted and cooled
1 egg
1 tablespoon milk
½ teaspoon vanilla
   Apricot Mini Muffin Mix

1. Preheat oven to 350°F. Spray 12 mini (1¾-inch) muffin cups with nonstick cooking spray; set aside.

2. Whisk together butter, egg, milk, and vanilla in medium bowl. Add muffin mix; stir until smooth. Spoon about 1 tablespoon batter into each prepared muffin cup.

3. Bake 12 to 15 minutes or until toothpick inserted into centers comes out clean.

Makes 12 mini muffins

Cranberry White Chocolate Drops Mix

½ cup plus 2 tablespoons all-purpose flour
¼ cup packed brown sugar
¼ cup white chocolate chips
¼ cup dried cranberries
 2 tablespoons granulated sugar
¼ teaspoon baking soda
⅛ teaspoon salt

1. Combine all ingredients in small bowl. Spoon into small food storage bag. Seal; place in 1½-cup mug.

2. Decorate mug and attach gift tag with preparation instructions.

Makes 1 mix

Cranberry White Chocolate Drops

¼ cup (½ stick) butter, softened
 1 egg
¾ teaspoon vanilla
   Cranberry White Chocolate Drops Mix

1. Preheat oven to 375°F. Beat butter in medium bowl with electric mixer at medium speed until creamy. Add egg and vanilla; beat until well blended. (Mixture may look curdled.)

2. Add cookie mix; beat until blended. Drop dough by tablespoonfuls onto ungreased cookie sheet.

3. Bake 8 to 10 minutes or until golden brown. Cool cookies on cookie sheet 1 minute; remove to wire rack to cool completely.

Makes about 14 cookies

Pumpkin Bread Mix

⅓ cup all-purpose flour
2 tablespoons granulated sugar
1 tablespoon packed brown sugar
1 tablespoon currants
1 teaspoon baking powder
½ teaspoon pumpkin pie spice or ground cinnamon
⅛ teaspoon salt
¼ cup powdered sugar

1. Mix flour, granulated sugar, brown sugar, currants, baking powder pumpkin pie spice and salt in small bowl. Spoon into small food storage bag. Seal; label "bread mix" and place in 1½-cup oven-safe mug. Spoon powdered sugar into separate small food storage bag. Seal; label "glaze mix" and place in mug.

2. Decorate mug and attach gift tag with preparation instructions.

Makes 1 mix

Pumpkin Bread

Pumpkin Bread Mix
3 tablespoons canned solid-pack pumpkin
1 egg
1 tablespoon vegetable oil
1 teaspoon lemon juice or water

1. Preheat oven to 350°F. Spray inside of mug with nonstick cooking spray. Place mug on baking sheet.

2. Combine bread mix, pumpkin, egg and oil in small bowl; stir until well blended. Pour batter into prepared mug.

3. Bake 30 minutes or until toothpick inserted into center comes out clean. Add lemon juice to glaze mix bag; seal and knead until blended. Cut small corner from bag; drizzle glaze over bread.

Makes 1 to 2 servings

Rice Pudding Mix

⅔ cup uncooked instant rice
⅓ cup nonfat dry milk powder
2 tablespoons sugar
2 tablespoons raisins
1 tablespoon cornstarch
⅛ teaspoon ground cinnamon
Pinch salt

1. Combine all ingredients in small bowl. Spoon into small food storage bag. Seal; place in 1½-cup microwave-safe mug.

2. Decorate mug and attach gift tag with preparation instructions.

Makes 1 mix

Rice Pudding

Rice Pudding Mix
¾ cup boiling water
⅛ teaspoon ground cinnamon

1. Empty pudding mix into mug; gradually add water, stirring to mix well.

2. Cover mug with vented plastic wrap. Microwave on HIGH 1 minute. Let stand, covered, 5 minutes. Stir before serving and sprinkle with cinnamon.

Makes 1 serving

Asian Noodle Soup Mix

**½ (3-ounce) package ramen noodles, including half of
    seasoning packet**
1 teaspoon dried chives
¼ teaspoon sesame seeds
¼ teaspoon granulated garlic
⅛ teaspoon ground ginger

1. Break noodles into chunks and place in small bowl. Sprinkle half of noodle seasoning packet, chives, sesame seeds, garlic and ginger over noodles. (Save remaining noodles and seasoning for another use.) Spoon mixture into small food storage bag. Seal; place in 1½-cup mug.

2. Decorate mug and attach gift tag with preparation instructions.

Makes 1 mix

Asian Noodle Soup

1½ cups water
Asian Noodle Soup Mix
½ cup fresh or frozen snow peas or sugar snap peas

1. Heat water in small saucepan over high heat until boiling. Add soup mix and peas; stir until blended.

2. Reduce heat to medium; simmer 3 minutes or until noodles are tender.

Makes 1 serving

Date Nut Bread Mix

⅔ cup all-purpose flour
¼ cup chopped dried dates (about 6 dates)
3 tablespoons sugar
2 tablespoons chopped walnuts
¼ teaspoon ground cinnamon
¼ teaspoon ground ginger
⅛ teaspoon baking powder
⅛ teaspoon baking soda
Pinch salt

1. Combine all ingredients in small bowl. Spoon into small food storage bag. Seal; place in 1½-cup mug.

2. Decorate mug and attach gift tag with preparation instructions.

Makes 1 mix

Date Nut Bread

¼ cup milk
3 tablespoons vegetable oil
1 egg
Date Nut Bread Mix

1. Preheat oven to 350°F. Spray mini (5½×3-inch) loaf pan with nonstick cooking spray; set aside.

2. Whisk milk, oil and egg together in medium bowl until smooth. Add bread mix; stir until well blended and smooth.

3. Spoon batter into prepared pan. Bake 35 to 40 minutes or until toothpick inserted into center comes out clean. Cool in pan on wire rack 10 minutes. Remove from pan; cool completely on wire rack.

Makes 2 to 3 servings

No-Bake Haystack Cookie Mix

1 cup (6 ounces) semisweet chocolate chips
1 cup crisp chow mein noodles
¼ cup roasted peanuts
¼ cup shredded coconut
¼ cup raisins

1. Place chocolate chips in small food storage bag. Seal; place in 1½-cup microwave-safe mug. Combine chow mein noodles, peanuts, coconut and raisins in small bowl. Spoon into separate small food storage bag. Seal; place in mug.

2. Decorate mug and attach gift tag with preparation instructions.

Makes 1 mix

No-Bake Haystack Cookies

No-Bake Haystack Cookie Mix

1. Line small cookie sheet with waxed paper. Pour bag of chocolate chips into mug. Microwave on HIGH 15 seconds; stir. Repeat until chips are melted and smooth.

2. Pour chow mein noodle mixture into medium bowl. Pour melted chocolate over noodle mixture; stir until well coated. Drop mixture by rounded tablespoonfuls onto prepared cookie sheet. Refrigerate 1 hour or until set.

Makes 10 cookies

Chile-Rice Soup Mix

1 can (4 ounces) diced mild green chiles
1 cup uncooked instant rice
1 package (about 1½ ounces) tomato with basil dry soup mix
2 teaspoons chili powder
1 teaspoon ground cumin

1. Place unopened can of chiles in 1½-cup mug. Combine rice, tomato soup mix, chili powder and cumin in small bowl. Spoon into small food storage bag. Seal; place in mug.

2. Decorate mug and attach gift tag with preparation instructions.

Makes 1 mix

Chile-Rice Soup

Chile-Rice Soup Mix
3 cups water

1. Combine can of chiles, including liquid, and soup mix in medium saucepan. Add water; stir until well blended. Bring to a boil over medium-high heat.

2. Reduce heat to low; simmer, stirring occasionally, 5 minutes or until rice is tender. Serve immediately. (Soup thickens upon standing.)

Makes about 3 servings

Pineapple Upside-Down Mini Cake Mix

1 single serving container (4 ounces) pineapple tidbits packed in juice
½ cup all-purpose flour
½ teaspoon baking powder
Pinch salt
¼ cup packed brown sugar

1. Place container of pineapple in 2-cup* oven-safe mug. Combine flour, baking powder and salt in small bowl. Spoon into small food storage bag. Seal; label "cake mix" and place in mug. Place brown sugar in separate small food storage bag. Seal; label "topping mix" and place in mug.

2. Decorate mug and attach gift tag with preparation instructions.

Makes 1 mix

Do not use a smaller mug, or batter may overflow during baking.

Pineapple Upside-Down Mini Cake

1 tablespoon butter
Pineapple Upside-Down Mini Cake Mix
2 tablespoons plus 2 teaspoons granulated sugar
1½ tablespoons shortening
1 egg
3 tablespoons milk

1. Preheat oven to 350°F. Spray inside of 2-cup mug with nonstick cooking spray. (Do not use smaller mug, or batter may overflow.)

2. Place butter and topping mix in bottom of mug. Microwave on HIGH 1 minute; stir until well blended. Drain pineapple; add to mug. Set aside.

3. Place granulated sugar and shortening in small bowl. Press ingredients together on side of bowl with large spoon until light and creamy. Add egg; stir until well blended. Add cake mix; stir until well blended. Add milk; stir until smooth. Pour into mug. Place mug on baking sheet.

4. Bake about 30 minutes or until toothpick inserted into center comes out clean. Cool 5 minutes on wire rack. Invert onto serving plate.

Makes 2 servings

Creamy Potato-Bacon Soup Mix

½ cup instant mashed potato flakes
2 tablespoons nonfat dry milk powder
1 tablespoon imitation bacon bits
1 teaspoon dried celery flakes
1 teaspoon chicken bouillon granules
½ teaspoon onion powder
⅛ teaspoon black pepper

1. Combine all ingredients in small bowl. Spoon into small food storage bag. Seal; place in 1½-cup microwave-safe mug.

2. Decorate mug and attach gift tag with preparation instructions.

Makes 1 mix

Creamy Potato-Bacon Soup

1¼ cups water
Creamy Potato-Bacon Soup Mix

1. Combine water and soup mix in mug; stir until well blended.

2. Cover mug with vented plastic wrap. Microwave on HIGH 3 minutes. Stir well before serving.

Makes 1 serving

Banana Chocolate Chip Bread Mix

¼ cup all-purpose flour
2 tablespoons sugar
4 tablespoons mini chocolate chips, divided
1 tablespoon finely chopped walnuts
¼ teaspoon baking soda
⅛ teaspoon ground cinnamon
Pinch salt

1. Mix flour, sugar, 2 tablespoons chocolate chips, walnuts, baking soda, cinnamon and salt in small bowl. Spoon into small food storage bag. Seal; label "bread mix" and place in 1½-cup oven-safe mug. Spoon remaining 2 tablespoons chips into separate small food storage bag. Seal; label "glaze" and place in mug.

2. Decorate mug and attach gift tag with preparation instructions.

Makes 1 mix

Banana Chocolate Chip Bread

½ ripe banana, chopped (about ¼ cup)
1 tablespoon oil
1 egg
Banana Chocolate Chip Bread Mix

1. Preheat oven to 350°F. Spray inside of mug with nonstick cooking spray. Place mug on baking sheet.

2. Place banana in small bowl. Mash banana with oil and egg. Add bread mix; stir until well blended.

3. Pour batter into prepared mug. Bake 25 minutes or until top springs back when gently touched.

4. Place sealed glaze bag in microwave; cook on MEDIUM-HIGH (70%) 30 to 45 seconds or until chips melt. Knead bag until chocolate is smooth. Cut small corner from bag; drizzle glaze over bread.

Makes 1 to 2 servings

Banana Chocolate Chip Bread

Preheat oven to 90 degrees.
Spray inside of mug with cooking spray. Prepare
mash banana with oil & egg...
diced banana in a small bowl... with the fork for
Pour batter into mug & top... stir in dry cook at back
when touched. Sprinkle chips high... lay the bread
at 2 minutes to soften...

The publisher would like to thank the companies and organizations listed below for the use of their recipes and photographs in this publication.

ACH Food Companies, Inc.

California Dried Plum Board

Duncan Hines® and Moist Deluxe® are registered trademarks of Pinnacle Foods Corp.

EAGLE BRAND®

The Hershey Company

© Mars, Incorporated 2007

National Honey Board

Nestlé USA

The Quaker® Oatmeal Kitchens

Reckitt Benckiser Inc.

VOLUME MEASUREMENTS (dry)

1/8 teaspoon = 0.5 mL
1/4 teaspoon = 1 mL
1/2 teaspoon = 2 mL
3/4 teaspoon = 4 mL
1 teaspoon = 5 mL
1 tablespoon = 15 mL
2 tablespoons = 30 mL
1/4 cup = 60 mL
1/3 cup = 75 mL
1/2 cup = 125 mL
2/3 cup = 150 mL
3/4 cup = 175 mL
1 cup = 250 mL
2 cups = 1 pint = 500 mL
3 cups = 750 mL
4 cups = 1 quart = 1 L

VOLUME MEASUREMENTS (fluid)

1 fluid ounce (2 tablespoons) = 30 mL
4 fluid ounces (1/2 cup) = 125 mL
8 fluid ounces (1 cup) = 250 mL
12 fluid ounces (1 1/2 cups) = 375 mL
16 fluid ounces (2 cups) = 500 mL

WEIGHTS (mass)

1/2 ounce = 15 g
1 ounce = 30 g
3 ounces = 90 g
4 ounces = 120 g
8 ounces = 225 g
10 ounces = 285 g
12 ounces = 360 g
16 ounces = 1 pound = 450 g

DIMENSIONS

1/16 inch = 2 mm
1/8 inch = 3 mm
1/4 inch = 6 mm
1/2 inch = 1.5 cm
3/4 inch = 2 cm
1 inch = 2.5 cm

OVEN TEMPERATURES

250°F = 120°C
275°F = 140°C
300°F = 150°C
325°F = 160°C
350°F = 180°C
375°F = 190°C
400°F = 200°C
425°F = 220°C
450°F = 230°C

BAKING PAN SIZES

Utensil	Size in Inches/Quarts	Metric Volume	Size in Centimeters
Baking or Cake Pan (square or rectangular)	8×8×2	2 L	20×20×5
	9×9×2	2.5 L	23×23×5
	12×8×2	3 L	30×20×5
	13×9×2	3.5 L	33×23×5
Loaf Pan	8×4×3	1.5 L	20×10×7
	9×5×3	2 L	23×13×7
Round Layer Cake Pan	8×1½	1.2 L	20×4
	9×1½	1.5 L	23×4
Pie Plate	8×1¼	750 mL	20×3
	9×1¼	1 L	23×3
Baking Dish or Casserole	1 quart	1 L	—
	1½ quart	1.5 L	—
	2 quart	2 L	—